SCHOLASTIC

# BOOK OF WORLD RECORDS 2018

BY
CYNTHIA O'BRIEN
ABIGAIL MITCHELL
MICHAEL BRIGHT
DONALD SOMMERVILLE

Due to this book's publication date, the majority of statistics are current as of May 2017. The publisher does not have any control over and does not assume any responsibility for author or third-party websites or their content.

This book was created and produced by Toucan Books Limited.
Text: Cynthia O'Brien, Abigail Mitchell, Michael Bright, Donald Sommerville
Designer: Lee Riches
Editor: Anna Southgate
Proofreader: Marion Dent
Index: Marie Lorimer
Toucan would like to thank Cian O'Day for picture research.

ISBN 978-1-338-19005-2

10 9 8 7 6 5 4 3 2 1    17 18 19 20 21

Printed in the U.S.A. 40

First printing 2017

# CONTENTS

**1**

MUSIC MAKERS

# MUSIC MAKERS
# TRENDING ⤴#

## QUEEN OF KARAOKE
### The First Lady takes a ride

A number of big names have joined *Late Late Show* host James Corden for his Carpool Karaoke segment, leading to some truly memorable videos. His segment with singing sensation Adele went viral in January 2016, racking up 136 million views on YouTube by the end of the year, but she was not the show's most surprising guest star. In July, First Lady Michelle Obama took to Corden's car to sing, rap, and dance, joined by rapper Missy Elliott.

## #FORMATION
### Biggest surprise album drop

Beyoncé dropped her visual album *Lemonade* on April 23, 2016—prompting a massive 4.1 million tweets in under forty-eight hours. It was released with little fanfare, but the power of surprise marketing combined with Queen Bey's talent and stardom made it one of the top-selling albums of 2016. *Lemonade* first aired on HBO as a complete film, although the music videos for each song on the album can be viewed separately.

## IN THE MOOD
Top streamed songs on Spotify

According to Spotify's 2016 review, the most streamed sad song of 2016 was "Say Something" by A Great Big World. In contrast, the top streamed party song was the 2015 hit "Uptown Funk!" by Mark Ronson, featuring Bruno Mars. The top song for listening while playing games was "Remember the Name" by underground hip-hop collaborators Fort Minor and Styles of Beyond. The streaming giant also announced that November 11, 2016, was the year's "most musical day."

## ACA-MAZING
Unexpected collaborators

In 2017, a cappella group Pentatonix earned their third Grammy for a collaboration with country music legend Dolly Parton, after remixing her iconic 1973 hit "Jolene." Pentatonix—comprised of singers Scott Hoying, Mitch Grassi, Kirstin Maldonado, Avi Kaplan, and Kevin Olusola—performed the song with both Parton and her goddaughter Miley Cyrus to critical acclaim on the hit show *The Voice* in November 2016. Videos of their performance went viral across social media.

## BREAKOUT TALENT
Young star goes viral

*America's Got Talent* contestant Grace VanderWaal achieved viral fame in 2016 for her performance of an original song, "I Don't Know My Name," accompanied by a ukulele. The twelve-year-old talent received a "golden buzzer," sending her straight through to the live rounds, and saw the video of her audition hit sixty million views. VanderWaal has since gained an impressive list of celebrity fans— and she even counts Taylor Swift among her Twitter followers.

## MOST DOWNLOADED song "CAN'T STOP THE FEELING!"

Only five songs released in 2016 had more than two million downloads, and topping this list was Justin Timberlake's peppy summer anthem "Can't Stop the Feeling!" The song, which was written for the 2016 DreamWorks movie *Trolls*, bounced to the top of the charts and won Timberlake his first Academy Award nomination for Best Song. Not only did Timberlake write the hit—and several others—for *Trolls* but he also voiced the character of grumpy troll Branch and served as the movie's executive music producer.

## MOST DOWNLOADED SONGS 2016
Units sold, in millions

Justin Timberlake, "Can't Stop the Feeling!" 2,495,000

The Chainsmokers, featuring Halsey, "Closer" 2,268,000

Flo Rida, "My House" 2,241,000

Lukas Graham, "7 Years" 2,113,000

Drake, featuring WizKid & Kyla, "One Dance" 2,008,000

# TOP-SELLING album 25

Adele's *25* took the title of top-selling album for the second year in a row, with 1.73 million copies sold in 2016. Adele's previous album, *21*, also spent two years as top-selling album in 2011 and 2012, earning $5.82 million the first year and $4.41 million the second. While

Adele reigned supreme in terms of traditional album sales, when it came to equivalent album units—a metric that includes track equivalent and streaming equivalent albums—*25* was bested by Drake's *Views*, with a huge 4.14 million albums sold compared to *25*'s 2.37 million.

## TOP-SELLING ALBUMS 2016
U.S. sales in millions of U.S. dollars

Adele, *25* 1.73

Drake, *Views* 1.60

Beyoncé, *Lemonade* 1.55

Chris Stapleton, *Traveller* 1.10

Twenty One Pilots
*Blurryface* 0.74

# MOST DOWNLOADED
# song in one week

Adele's song "Hello" shot to the top of the charts after its release on October 23, 2015, with over 1.1 million downloads in the United States in just one week. It is the first song ever to reach that total in such a short time. On YouTube, the video for "Hello" had 27.7 million views in twenty-four hours, breaking Taylor Swift's record. "Hello" was released almost a month ahead of the long-awaited *25*, Adele's follow-up album to her mega hit *21*.

# "HELLO"

# TOP-EARNING
# tour BRUCE
# SPRINGSTEEN

Bruce Springsteen & the E Street Band earned the title of 2016's bestselling tour, with shows celebrating the thirty-fifth anniversary of his 1980 album *The River*. The tour brought in $268.3 million worldwide. Each show of the tour was three hours and twenty minutes long—proving that age had not slowed down the then sixty-seven-year-old Springsteen. The band played not only songs from *The River*, but twelve other hits as well.

## TOP-EARNING TOURS 2016 (PER POLLSTAR)
In millions of U.S. dollars

Bruce Springsteen
**268.3**

Beyoncé
**256.4**

Coldplay
**241**

Guns N' Roses
**188.4**

Adele
**167.7**

# FIRST RAPPER TO TOP
# Billboard 100 chart
# DRAKE

Drake released his album *If You're Reading This It's Too Late* through iTunes on February 12, 2015. The digital album sold 495,000 units in its first week and entered the *Billboard* 100 at no. 1, making Drake the first rap artist ever to top the chart. The album also helped Drake secure another record: the most hits on the *Billboard* 100 at one time.

On March 7, 2015, Drake had fourteen hit songs on the chart, matching the record the Beatles have held since 1964. Since releasing his first hit single, "Best I Ever Had," in 2009, Drake has seen many of his singles go multiplatinum, including "Hotline Bling," which sold 41,000 copies in its first week and had 18 weeks at no. 1 on the *Billboard* 100.

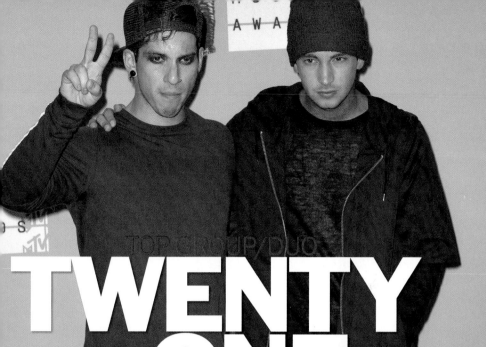

# TWENTY ONE PILOTS

Singing duo Tyler Joseph and Josh Dun, who perform under the name Twenty One Pilots, were the number one group/duo of 2016, according to *Billboard*. The Ohio natives had a strong year: Their album *Blurryface* sold 738,000 copies, making them the only group on the *Billboard* top-ten albums list. *Blurryface* also beat out the late David Bowie's *Blackstar* as the album with the most sales on vinyl, selling 68,000 copies. In August, the duo made history when their singles "Ride" and "Heathens"— from the soundtrack to DC's *Suicide Squad*—simultaneously reached number one on the *Billboard* Pop and Alternative Songs charts, respectively.

## TOP FIVE GROUPS/DUOS 2016
1 Twenty One Pilots
2 Coldplay
3 The Chainsmokers
4 One Direction
5 Fifth Harmony

# TOP-SELLING recording THE group BEATLES

## TOP-SELLING RECORDING GROUPS IN THE UNITED STATES
Albums sold in millions

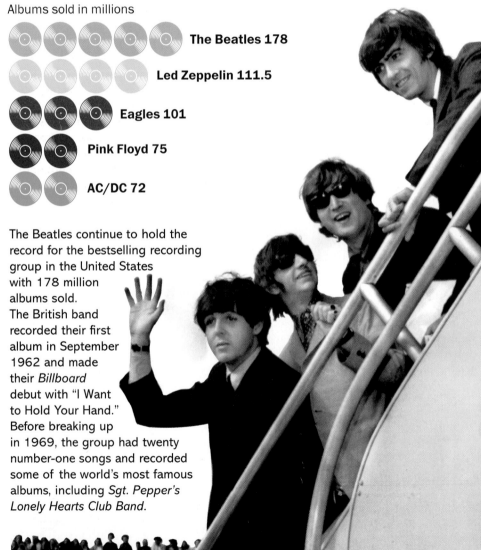

The Beatles 178

Led Zeppelin 111.5

Eagles 101

Pink Floyd 75

AC/DC 72

The Beatles continue to hold the record for the bestselling recording group in the United States with 178 million albums sold. The British band recorded their first album in September 1962 and made their *Billboard* debut with "I Want to Hold Your Hand." Before breaking up in 1969, the group had twenty number-one songs and recorded some of the world's most famous albums, including *Sgt. Pepper's Lonely Hearts Club Band*.

# SHORTEST CONCERT ever
# WHITE STRIPES

In St. John's, Newfoundland, the White Stripes' lead, Jack White, played just one note—a C sharp. The White Stripes had played at least one show in each of Canada's thirteen provinces and territories, as well as "secret" shows in various venues. Die-hard fans found out about these secret shows through posts on the White Stripes messageboard, The Little Room.

The one-note show in Newfoundland was a secret event, though hundreds turned up to watch. The official end of the tour was a full set played later that night. *Under Great White Northern Lights*, released in 2010, is a documentary of the tour. The film features backstage moments as well as scenes from the live concerts, and an impromptu performance on a public bus.

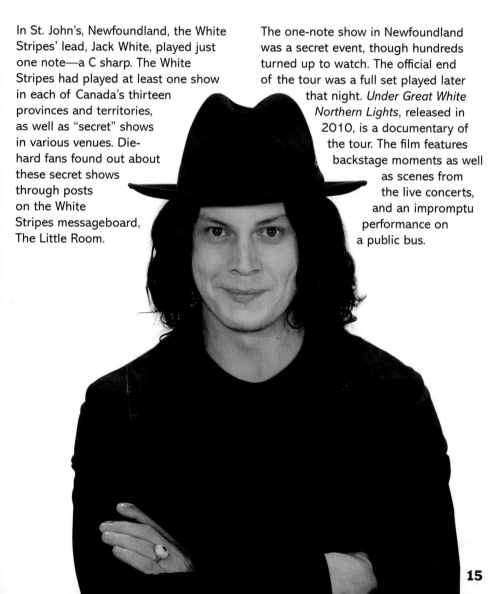

# BESTSELLING digital song of all time

# "BABY"

Justin Bieber's hit single "Baby" has sold twelve million copies since its release in March 2010. "Baby," featuring rapper Ludacris, appeared on Bieber's debut studio album, *My World*, which was nominated for a Grammy Award in 2011. Bieber began his career singing in videos on YouTube before he was discovered by a talent agent and offered a recording contract. His first single, "One Time," went platinum in January 2010, having sold one million copies since its release in June 2009. Bieber's latest album, *Purpose*, went platinum just three weeks after its release.

## BESTSELLING DIGITAL SONGS IN THE UNITED STATES
Units sold, in millions

**Justin Bieber, ft. Ludacris, "Baby" 12**

**Eminem, ft. Rihanna, "Love the Way You Lie" 11**

**Lady Gaga, "Bad Romance" 11**

**Imagine Dragons, "Radioactive" 10**

**Katy Perry, "Dark Horse" 10**

# LONGEST-EVER
# music video

# "HAPPY"
## BY PHARRELL

Pharrell Williams made history in November 2013 with the release of the first 24-hour music video—the longest music video ever. The video for Williams's hit song "Happy" is a four-minute track that plays on a loop 360 times. In addition to Williams, celebrities such as Jamie Foxx, Steve Carell, and Miranda Cosgrove make appearances in the video. In 2014, "Happy" broke records again, becoming the first single to top six *Billboard* charts in one year and becoming the year's bestselling song with 6,455,000 digital copies sold.

# TOP-EARNING female singer
# TAYLOR SWIFT

## TOP-EARNING FEMALE SINGERS 2016
In millions of U.S. dollars

Taylor Swift $170

Adele $80.5

Madonna $76.5

Rihanna $75

Beyoncé $54

Country-princess-turned-pop-megastar Taylor Swift earned more than double that of her closest competition, Adele, in 2016, raking in a gigantic $170 million. A huge chunk of Swift's income came from the 1989 World Tour, which finished in December 2015, with the rest coming from album sales and lucrative contracts with major brands such as Keds, Diet Coke, and Apple. Taylor Swift's record is doubly impressive, considering that she performed live only once in 2016—at the U.S. Grand Prix—and released no new music.

# TOP radio song "LOVE YOURSELF"

Canadian pop star Justin Bieber had the most played song on U.S. radio in 2016, with his monster hit "Love Yourself," which garnered 3.950 billion audience impressions. The figure factors in the number of times the song was heard by radio listeners. "Love Yourself" also had the most single radio plays, with 664,000 plays of the track. Bieber was a popular figure on the radio in 2016, with his song "Sorry" also making the top ten in radio audience impressions. Both songs were released on Bieber's 2015 album *Purpose*.

**TOP TEN RADIO SONGS IN THE U.S., 2016**
Number of audience impressions in billions

Justin Bieber, "Love Yourself" 3.950

Drake, ft. WizKid & Kyla, "One Dance" 3.611

Justin Timberlake, "Can't Stop the Feeling!" 3.422

Sia, ft. Sean Paul, "Cheap Thrills" 3.385

Twenty One Pilots, "Stressed Out" 3.369

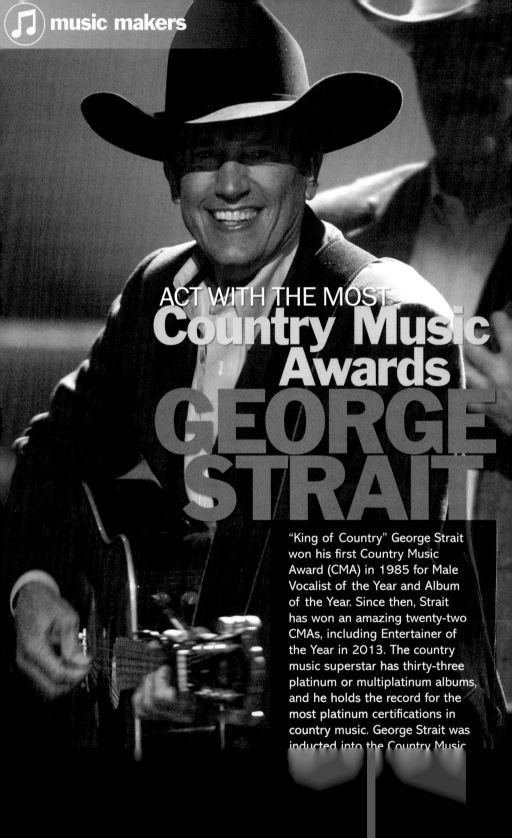

## ACT WITH THE MOST
# Country Music Awards
# GEORGE STRAIT

"King of Country" George Strait won his first Country Music Award (CMA) in 1985 for Male Vocalist of the Year and Album of the Year. Since then, Strait has won an amazing twenty-two CMAs, including Entertainer of the Year in 2013. The country music superstar has thirty-three platinum or multiplatinum albums, and he holds the record for the most platinum certifications in country music. George Strait was inducted into the Country Music

# MUSICIAN WITH THE MOST MTV Video Music Awards "
# BEYONCÉ

2016 was quite the year for queen of pop Beyoncé, who won eight MTV Video Music Awards in total, crowning her the winningest VMA artist ever. She surpassed Madonna's twenty VMA trophies to set a record of twenty-four VMA wins. The music video for "Formation," from Beyoncé's visual album *Lemonade*, won five awards, including the coveted prize for Video of the Year. With eight moon men from eleven nominations, Beyonce tied the record for the most VMA wins in one year by a female solo artist, also held by

## MUSICIAN WITH THE MOST MTV VIDEO MUSIC AWARDS

Beyoncé 24

Madonna 20

Lady Gaga 13

Peter Gabriel 13

Eminem 12

**MOST DOWNLOADED**
## country song
# "H.O.L.Y."

**Florida Georgia Line, "H.O.L.Y." 1,379,000**

**Tim McGraw, "Humble and Kind" 1,023,000**

**Thomas Rhett, "Die a Happy Man" 910,000**

**Maren Morris, "My Church" 830,000**

 **Dierks Bentley, "Somewhere on a Beach" 697,000**

**TOP-SELLING COUNTRY DIGITAL SONGS 2016**
Number of units sold

Country duo Florida Georgia Line (Brian Kelley, from Ormond Beach, Florida, and Tyler Hubbard, from Monroe, Georgia) released their third studio album, *Dig Your Roots*, in August 2016, and its lead single "H.O.L.Y." went to number one on the *Billboard* Country chart. The song, written by busbee, Nate Cyphert, and William Wiik Larsen, went on to become the most downloaded country song of the year, despite being more somber than the duo's usual lighthearted "bro country" tunes.

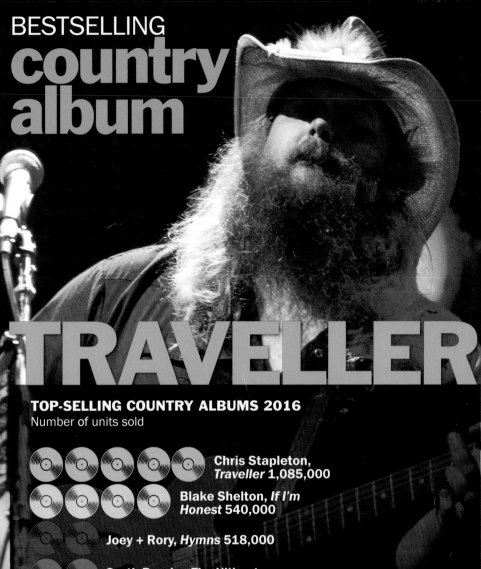

# BESTSELLING
# country album

# TRAVELLER

## TOP-SELLING COUNTRY ALBUMS 2016
Number of units sold

Chris Stapleton, *Traveller* 1,085,000

Blake Shelton, *If I'm Honest* 540,000

Joey + Rory, *Hymns* 518,000

Garth Brooks, *The Ultimate Collection* 421,000

Keith Urban, *Ripcord* 412,000

After years of experience writing contemporary country hits for other artists—such as Thomas Rhett's upbeat "Crash and Burn"—Chris Stapleton released his first studio album in 2015 to critical acclaim. *Traveller* subsequently sold over one million copies in 2016—the only country album to do so, and the only one to make the *Billboard* top-ten bestseller list. Stapleton wrote twelve of the fourteen tracks on the album, which draws heavily on the thirty-seven-year-old singer's influences for a sound reminiscent of 1970s country classics.

# 2

# screen & STAGE

# SCREEN & STAGE
# TRENDING #

## STRANGER THAN FICTION
### Best new streaming show

Netflix's sci-fi sensation *Stranger Things*, which debuted in 2016, quickly became the service's third most streamed show of all time, despite being in just its first season. Within its first thirty-five days online, *Stranger Things* is thought to have averaged over fourteen million viewers between the ages of eighteen and forty-nine.

## THE SHOW MUST GO ON
### The end of #Ham4Ham

Until September 2016, stars of the hit musical *Hamilton* delighted fans waiting outside the Richard Rodgers Theatre in New York City with impromptu performances. "Ham4Ham" took place during the live $10 ticket lottery, which brought thousands of people to West Forty-Sixth Street hoping to score coveted seats to the popular musical. The off-the-cuff shows soon made it onto YouTube, with one clip—"The Schuyler Georges"—surpassing one million views. The video features three of the Hamilton actors who played King George III covering "The Schuyler Sisters," a song usually sung by female cast members.

## LIVE COMMENTARY
Most tweeted show

Zombie-apocalypse drama *The Walking Dead* was the most live-tweeted show of the 2015–2016 season, with Nielsen reporting 435,000 tweets per episode. The Twittersphere was especially vocal after the Season 6 cliffhanger finale, which left fans wondering which of their favorite characters had been killed. Spoiler alert: Twitter fell into a frenzy once again when the Season 7 premiere revealed that not one but two of the main characters had met their end.

## TRUE LOVE?
Most tweeted reality show

Dating show *The Bachelor* beat out singing contest *The Voice* as the most tweeted reality show of the 2015–2016 season, with 248,000 tweets per episode on average. In 2016 the ABC show aired its twentieth season, which followed twenty-six-year-old Ben Higgins on his journey to find love, with fans online speculating whether Lauren Bushnell or JoJo Fletcher would get the "final rose."

## #FINALLY
First Oscar for Leonardo DiCaprio

It was a sad day for Tumblr when Leonardo DiCaprio finally won an Academy Award; the microblogging site collectively mourned the end of a popular meme. While many on social media celebrated the actor's win for *The Revenant*—which came after more than twenty years in Hollywood and five previous Oscar nominations—the official account for Tumblr took a different tone, posting "RIP Leo Gets Snubbed By Oscars Meme: 1994–2016."

# LONGEST-RUNNING
# scripted TV show in the United States
# THE SIMPSONS

MATT GROENING

In 2016, *The Simpsons* entered a record twenty-eighth season, making it the longest-running American sitcom, cartoon, and scripted prime-time television show in history. The animated comedy, which first aired in December 1989, centers on the antics and everyday lives of the Simpson family. The show's creator, Matt Groening, named the characters after members in his own family, although he substituted Bart for his own name. In 2016, the show's guest stars included Drew Carey and Wayne Gretzky.

# TV SHOW WITH THE MOST
## Emmy Awards
# SATURDAY NIGHT LIVE

The variety show *Saturday Night Live* has won forty-five Emmy Awards since it premiered in 1975. The late-night comedy show broadcasts live from New York City's Rockefeller Center on Saturday nights. A new celebrity host introduces the show each week and takes part in comedy skits with the regular cast. *Saturday Night Live* launched the careers of America's top comedians, including Will Ferrell, Tina Fey, and Kristen Wiig, many of whom return to the show regularly in guest spots. In 2016, Kate McKinnon made history when she became the first *SNL* cast member to win an Emmy for Supporting Actress in a Comedy. Throughout 2016, McKinnon famously impersonated Democratic presidential candidate Hillary Clinton on the show.

# HIGHEST-PAID
# TV actress SOFÍA VERGARA

In 2016, *Modern Family*'s Sofía Vergara beat out *Big Bang Theory*'s Kaley Cuoco to become not only the highest-paid actress on television, but the highest-paid small-screen star in Hollywood. The actress earned $43 million in 2016—a 66 percent bump from 2015, thanks to her endorsement and licensing deals, including her own line of furniture and perfume. Vergara, who is originally from Colombia, has won four Screen Actors Guild Awards as part of the *Modern Family* cast for Outstanding Performance by an Ensemble in a Comedy Series.

## TOP-EARNING TV ACTRESSES
In millions of U.S. dollars

Sofía Vergara $43

Kaley Cuoco $24.5

Mindy Kaling $15
Ellen Pompeo $14.5

Mariska Hargitay $14.5

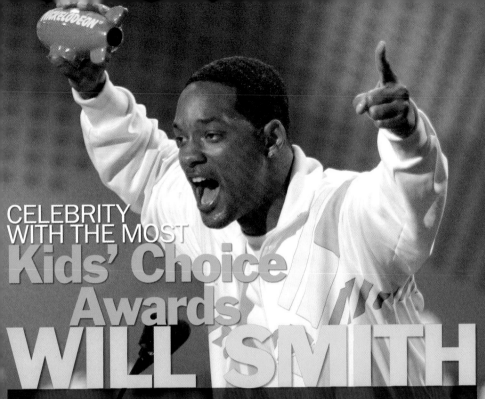

# CELEBRITY WITH THE MOST
## Kids' Choice Awards
## WILL SMITH

Will Smith has won 11 Kids' Choice Awards, including two Best Actor wins for his roles in *The Fresh Prince of Bel-Air* and *Hancock*. Will Smith's career took off with *The Fresh Prince of Bel-Air*, a sitcom that aired for six years in the 1990s. He went on to have a highly successful movie career, earning two Academy Award nominations for *The Pursuit of Happyness* and *Ali*. Nickelodeon introduced the Kids' Choice Awards in 1988—a highlight of the show is its tradition of "sliming" celebrity guests with green goo, often taking them by surprise.

## CELEBRITIES WITH THE MOST KIDS' CHOICE AWARDS

Will Smith 11

Adam Sandler 10

Selena Gomez 9

Miley Cyrus 6

Amanda Bynes 6

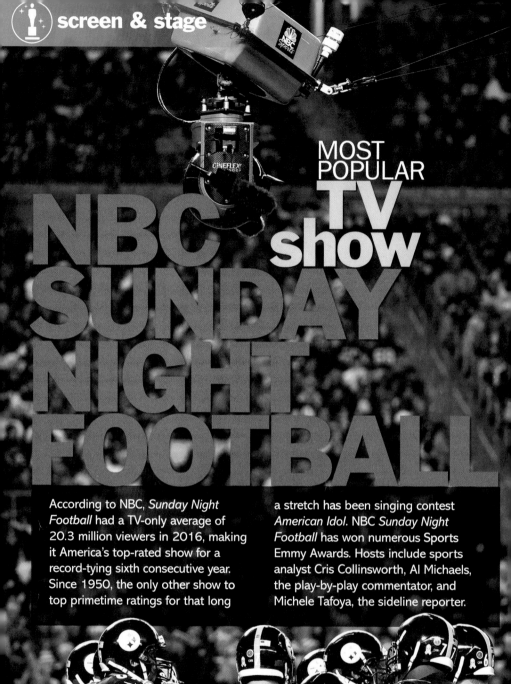

# NBC SUNDAY NIGHT FOOTBALL

## MOST POPULAR TV show

According to NBC, *Sunday Night Football* had a TV-only average of 20.3 million viewers in 2016, making it America's top-rated show for a record-tying sixth consecutive year. Since 1950, the only other show to top primetime ratings for that long a stretch has been singing contest *American Idol*. NBC *Sunday Night Football* has won numerous Sports Emmy Awards. Hosts include sports analyst Cris Collinsworth, Al Michaels, the play-by-play commentator, and Michele Tafoya, the sideline reporter.

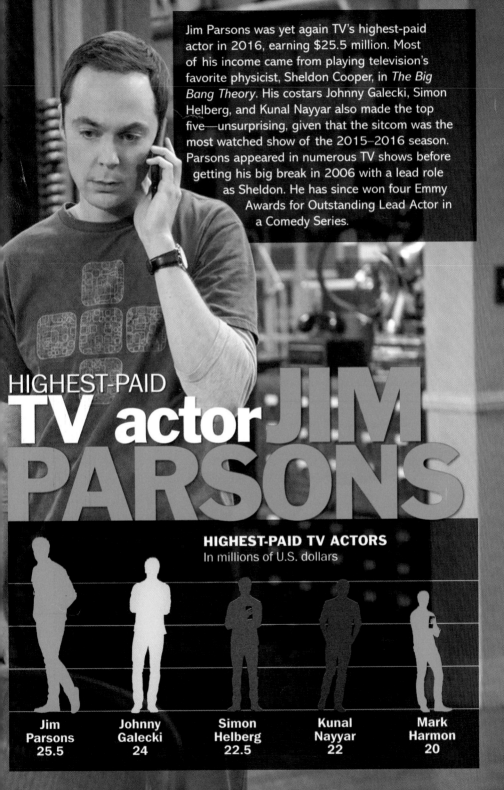

Jim Parsons was yet again TV's highest-paid actor in 2016, earning $25.5 million. Most of his income came from playing television's favorite physicist, Sheldon Cooper, in *The Big Bang Theory*. His costars Johnny Galecki, Simon Helberg, and Kunal Nayyar also made the top five—unsurprising, given that the sitcom was the most watched show of the 2015–2016 season. Parsons appeared in numerous TV shows before getting his big break in 2006 with a lead role as Sheldon. He has since won four Emmy Awards for Outstanding Lead Actor in a Comedy Series.

# HIGHEST-PAID
# TV actor JIM PARSONS

## HIGHEST-PAID TV ACTORS
In millions of U.S. dollars

| Jim Parsons | Johnny Galecki | Simon Helberg | Kunal Nayyar | Mark Harmon |
|---|---|---|---|---|
| 25.5 | 24 | 22.5 | 22 | 20 |

# MOVIE WITH THE HIGHEST production costs

## MOVIES WITH THE HIGHEST PRODUCTION COSTS
In millions of U.S. dollars

*Pirates of the Caribbean: On Stranger Tides 378.5*

*Pirates of the Caribbean: At World's End 300.0*

*Avengers: Age of Ultron 279.9*

*John Carter 263.7*

*Tangled 260.0*

*Pirates of the Caribbean: On Stranger Tides* cost a huge $378.5 million to produce, almost $80 million more than *Pirates of the Caribbean: At World's End*, released four years earlier. The 2011 movie was the fourth in Walt Disney's Pirates of the Caribbean franchise starring Johnny Depp as Captain Jack Sparrow. In this installment of the wildly popular series, Captain Jack goes in search of the Fountain of Youth. Depp earned $55.5 million for the role, and the movie went on to earn $1.04 billion worldwide. Johnny Depp returns to play Captain Jack in *Pirates of the Caribbean: Dead Men Tell No Tales*, the latest title in the franchise.

# PIRATES OF THE CARIBBEAN
# ON STRANGER TIDES

# MOST SUCCESSFUL movie franchise

# MARVEL CINEMATIC UNIVERSE

The Marvel Comics superhero movie franchise has grossed over $10 billion worldwide—and counting! *The Avengers*, released in 2012, is the top-grossing movie in the Marvel Cinematic Universe, having earned $1.52 billion worldwide. The movie features Marvel's best-loved superheroes, including Iron Man, played by Robert Downey Jr., and Captain America, played by Chris Evans. The Marvel franchise also includes blockbuster movies starring individual superheroes, such as *Iron Man, Thor, Ant-Man, Captain America*, and *The Incredible Hulk*.

**Marvel Cinematic Universe 10.91**

**Harry Potter 8.54**

**Star Wars 7.61**

**James Bond 7.08**

**Peter Jackson's Lord of the Rings 5.90**

**MOST SUCCESSFUL MOVIE FRANCHISES**
Total worldwide gross, in billions of U.S. dollars

# movies with the most
# OSCARS

## MOVIES WITH THE MOST OSCARS

*Ben-Hur* (1959) 11

*Titanic* (1997) 11

*The Lord of the Rings: The Return of the King* (2003) 11

*West Side Story* (1961) 10

*Gigi* (1958); *The Last Emperor* (1987); *The English Patient* (1996) 9

It's a three-way tie for the movie with the most Academy Awards: *Ben-Hur*, *Titanic*, and *The Lord of the Rings: The Return of the King* have each won eleven Oscars, including Best Picture and Best Director. The 1959 biblical epic *Ben-Hur* was the first to achieve this record number of wins. *Titanic*, based on the real 1912 disaster, won numerous Oscars for its striking visual and sound effects. *The Lord of the Rings: The Return of the King* was the third in a trilogy based on the books by J. R. R. Tolkien. It is the only movie of the top three to win in every category in which it was nominated.

## SO WHO'S OSCAR?

Every year the Academy of Motion Picture Arts and Sciences presents awards in recognition of the greatest achievements in the film industry. Those actors, directors, screenplay writers, and producers lucky enough to win each receive a highly prized golden statuette A.K.A. Oscar. No one really knows where the name comes from, although it is thought to have originated among the Hollywood greats of the 1930s—Bette Davis and Walt Disney have been credited, among others. Either way, Oscar became the official nickname for the Academy Award in 1939.

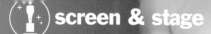

# YOUNGEST ACTRESS nominated for an Oscar

## QUVENZHANÉ WALLIS

At nine years old, Quvenzhané Wallis became the youngest-ever Academy Award nominee. The actress received the Best Actress nomination in 2013 for her role as Hushpuppy in *Beasts of the Southern Wild*. Although Wallis did not win the Oscar, she went on to gain forty-one more nominations and win twenty-four awards at various industry award shows. In 2015, she received a Golden Globe Best Actress nomination for her role in *Annie*. Wallis was five years old when she auditioned for Hushpuppy (the minimum age was six), and she won the part over four thousand other candidates.

Justin Henry was just seven years old when he received a Best Supporting Actor nomination for *Kramer vs. Kramer* in 1980. His neighbor, a casting director, suggested that Henry try out for the part. Although the young actor lost out on the Oscar, *Kramer vs. Kramer* won several Oscars, including Best Actor for Dustin Hoffman, Best Actress in a Supporting Role for Meryl Streep, and Best Picture. Justin Henry appeared in a few other films before leaving acting to finish his education. He then returned to acting in the 1990s.

YOUNGEST ACTOR
# nominated for an Oscar
# JUSTIN HENRY

# MOVIES WITH THE MOST SUCCESSFUL DOMESTIC OPENING WEEKEND

Weekend earnings, in millions of U.S. dollars

**Star Wars: The Force Awakens (12/18/15) 248.0**

**Jurassic World (6/12/15) 208.8**

**Marvel's The Avengers (5/4/12) 207.4**

**Avengers: Age of Ultron (5/1/15) 191.2**

**Captain America: Civil War (5/6/16) 179.1**

*Star Wars: Episode VII: The Force Awakens* broke box-office records in December 2015 as the movie with the most successful opening weekend in the United States and the movie that earned the most money in a single day. The movie's opening weekend of December 18–20, 2015 earned an incredible $247,966,675 in the United States and $528,966,675 worldwide. The film broke another record when it took just twelve days to reach $1 billion worldwide, faster than any film in history. On its opening day alone, *Star Wars: The Force Awakens* earned over $119 million. New stars Daisy Ridley, John Boyega, and Oscar Isaac joined original cast members Carrie Fisher, Harrison Ford, and Mark Hamill. Carrie Fisher, the actress who played Princess Leia, passed away in 2016, but not before filming scenes for the next movie in the franchise, *The Last Jedi*, due for release in December 2017. Following initial speculation over the future of Fisher's scenes in *The Last Jedi*, Disney filmmakers decided to leave them intact.

# STAR WARS: EPISODE VII: THE FORCE AWAKENS smashes

## BOX OFFICE RECORDS!

### STAR WARS STATS:

# 11,000,000

PRODUCTION COSTS FOR *STAR WARS: EPISODE IV: A NEW HOPE*: $11 million

# 245,000,000

PRODUCTION COSTS FOR *STAR WARS: EPISODE VII: THE FORCE AWAKENS*: $245 million

# 849,500,000

PRODUCTION COSTS FOR EIGHT STAR WARS MOVIES TO DATE: $849.5 million

# ACTRESSES WITH THE MOST
## MTV Movie Awards
# JENNIFER LAWRENCE
# AND KRISTEN STEWART

## ACTRESSES WITH THE MOST MTV MOVIE AWARDS

★★★★★ Jennifer Lawrence 7

★★★★★ Kristen Stewart 7

★★★ Shailene Woodley 5

★★ Sandra Bullock 4

★ Alicia Silverstone 4

Jennifer Lawrence and Kristen Stewart now share the title of actress with the most MTV Movie Awards. Stewart won all seven of her awards for her role as Bella Swan in the movie adaptations of the Twilight franchise—including four Best Kiss awards with costar Robert Pattinson. Lawrence's seventh award was for Best Hero, which she won in 2016 for her role as Katniss Everdeen in the fourth installment of the popular Hunger Games franchise. The actress, however, was a no-show at the awards ceremony in April, due to press commitments for her upcoming movie X-Men: Apocalypse.

# ACTOR WITH THE MOST

# JIM MTV Movie Awards CARREY

Jim Carrey has eleven MTV Movie Awards, including five Best Comedic Performance awards for his roles in *Dumb and Dumber* (1994), *Ace Ventura: When Nature Calls* (1995), *The Cable Guy* (1996), *Liar Liar* (1997), and *Yes Man* (2008). He won the Best Villain award twice, once for *The Cable Guy* (1996) and the second time for *Dr. Seuss' How the Grinch Stole Christmas* (2000). Fans also awarded Carrey with the Best Kiss award for his lip-lock with Lauren Holly in *Dumb and Dumber*.

## ACTORS WITH THE MOST MTV MOVIE AWARDS

★★★★★ Jim Carrey 11

★★★★ Robert Pattinson 10

★★★ Mike Myers 7

★★ Adam Sandler 6

★★ Will Smith 6

# TOP-EARNING
# actress
# JENNIFER LAWRENCE

Jennifer Lawrence earned a colossal $46 million in 2016. The actress, who played Katniss Everdeen in the smash-hit series The Hunger Games, took home a sizable chunk of the box-office profit for the final film in the franchise, *Mockingjay: Part 2*.

She also earned a huge upfront fee for space adventure *Passengers*, earning an impressive $20 million compared to costar Chris Pratt's $12 million. Lawrence's salary reportedly took up twenty percent of the film's entire budget.

## TOP-EARNING ACTRESSES
In millions of U.S. dollars

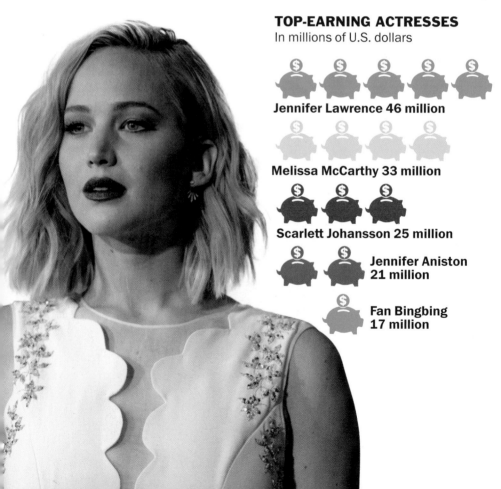

**Jennifer Lawrence 46 million**

**Melissa McCarthy 33 million**

**Scarlett Johansson 25 million**

**Jennifer Aniston 21 million**

**Fan Bingbing 17 million**

# TOP-EARNING actor
# THE ROCK

Former professional wrestler Dwayne "The Rock" Johnson earned a massive $64.5 million to win the title of top-earning film actor in 2016. Johnson, whose busy schedule for the year included such movies as *Central Intelligence*, *The Fate of the Furious*, and *Baywatch*, also starred as the main character in *Ballers*, a TV drama that wrapped shooting for its second season in March 2016. While the 6-foot-5-inch, 245-pound actor is known as an action hero, he also voiced the demigod Maui for Disney's *Moana*, released in 2016, and sang the catchy song "You're Welcome" for the movie's soundtrack.

## TOP-EARNING ACTORS
In millions of U.S. dollars

Dwayne Johnson 64.5

Jackie Chan 61

Matt Damon 55

Tom Cruise 53

Johnny Depp 48

# TOP-GROSSING movie CAPTAIN AMERICA: CIVIL WAR

Marvel added another hit to its cinematic universe in 2016 with the blockbuster *Captain America: Civil War*, the year's top-grossing movie. *Civil War* reported a massive $181.8-million opening weekend, knocking fellow Marvel movie *Iron Man 3* off the list of top five opening weekends ever. The third installment in Captain America's story stars familiar faces from the entire Avengers franchise—this time with its heroes pitted against each other. Chris Evans reprised his role as Captain America, with Robert Downey Jr.'s Iron Man leading the superhero opposition. *Civil War* also introduced new heroes from the comic books, such as Chadwick Boseman's Black Panther.

## TOP-GROSSING LIVE-ACTION MOVIES 2016
Worldwide gross in millions of U.S. dollars

*Captain America: Civil War* 1,153

*The Jungle Book* 966.6

*Batman v Superman: Dawn of Justice* 873.3

*Rogue One: A Star Wars Story* 801.9

*Deadpool* 783.1

# TOP-GROSSING
## animated film
# FINDING DORY

Pixar's follow-up to the 2003 hit *Finding Nemo* opened on June 17, 2016, and became not only the year's top-grossing animated movie, but Pixar's biggest opening weekend ever. *Finding Dory* grossed over $1 billion worldwide since its release, and is the fourth-highest-grossing animated movie of all time. *Finding Dory* stars the three main characters from the 2003 movie—Dory, Marlin, and Nemo—but this time tells the story of Dory's quest to find answers about her past. The movie won Ellen DeGeneres, who reprised her voice role as the forgetful fish, both a People's Choice Award and a Teen Choice Award.

## TOP-GROSSING ANIMATED MOVIES 2016
Worldwide gross in millions of U.S. dollars

Finding Dory 1,023
$

Zootopia 1,020
$  $

The Secret Life of Pets 876
$  $  $

Moana 580
$  $  $  $

Sing 550
$  $  $  $  $

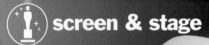
Andrew Lloyd Webber's *The Phantom of the Opera* opened on Broadway in January 1988 and has been performed more than 12,000 times. The original London cast members, Michael Crawford, Sarah Brightman, and Steve Barton, reprised their roles on Broadway. The story, based on a novel written in 1911 by French author Gaston Leroux, tells the tragic tale of the phantom and his love for an opera singer, Christine.

## LONGEST-RUNNING Broadway show THE PHANTOM OF THE OPERA

### LONGEST-RUNNING BROADWAY SHOWS

Total performances (as of January 2017)

 The Phantom of the Opera 12,035

Chicago (1996 Revival) 8,358

 The Lion King 7,971

 Cats 7,485

 Les Misérables 6,680

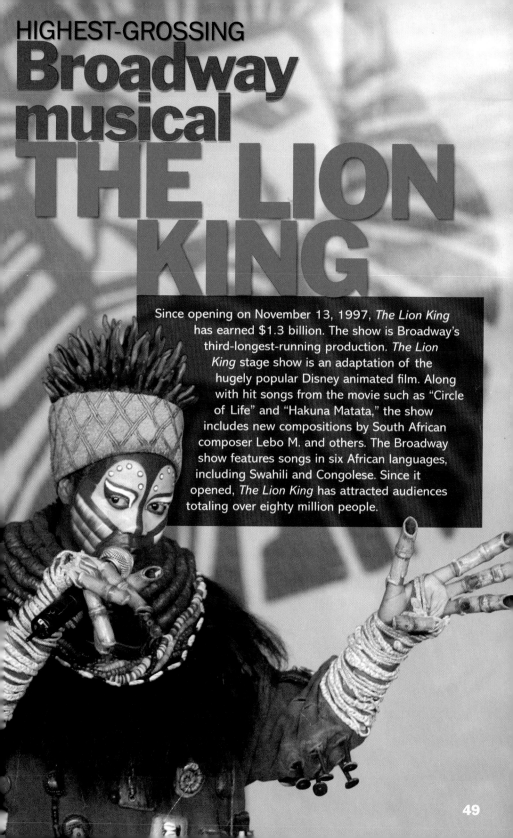

# HIGHEST-GROSSING
# Broadway musical
# THE LION KING

Since opening on November 13, 1997, *The Lion King* has earned $1.3 billion. The show is Broadway's third-longest-running production. *The Lion King* stage show is an adaptation of the hugely popular Disney animated film. Along with hit songs from the movie such as "Circle of Life" and "Hakuna Matata," the show includes new compositions by South African composer Lebo M. and others. The Broadway show features songs in six African languages, including Swahili and Congolese. Since it opened, *The Lion King* has attracted audiences totaling over eighty million people.

49

# MUSICAL WITH THE MOST Tony Award nominations HAMILTON

Lin-Manuel Miranda's musical biography of Founding Father Alexander Hamilton racked up an amazing sixteen Tony Award nominations to unseat the previous record holders, *The Producers* and *Billy Elliot, The Musical*, both of which had fifteen. The mega-hit hip-hop musical, which was inspired by historian Ron Chernow's biography of the first secretary of the treasury, portrays the Founding Fathers of the United States engaging in rap battles over issues such as the national debt and the French Revolution. *Hamilton* won eleven Tonys at the 2016 ceremony—one shy of *The Producers*, which retains the record for most Tony wins with twelve. *Hamilton*'s Broadway success paved the way for the show to open in Chicago in 2016, with a touring show and a London production planned for 2017.

# YOUNGEST WINNER
# of a Laurence Olivier Award

In 2012, four actresses shared an Olivier Award for their roles in the British production of *Matilda*. Eleanor Worthington-Cox, Cleo Demetriou, Kerry Ingram, and Sophia Kiely all won the award for Best Actress in a Musical. Of the four actresses, Worthington-Cox, age ten, was the youngest by a few weeks. Each actress portraying Matilda performs two shows a week. In the U.S., the four *Matilda* actresses won a special Tony Honors for Excellence in the Theater in 2013. *Matilda*, inspired by the book by Roald Dahl, won a record seven Olivier Awards in 2012.

ELEANOR WORTHINGTON-COX

CLEO DEMETRIOU

KERRY INGRAM

SOPHIA KIELY

on the MoVE

# ON THE MOVE
# TRENDING #

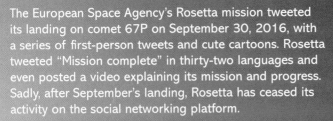

## FROM ROSETTA WITH LOVE
#CometLanding

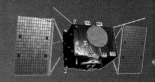

The European Space Agency's Rosetta mission tweeted its landing on comet 67P on September 30, 2016, with a series of first-person tweets and cute cartoons. Rosetta tweeted "Mission complete" in thirty-two languages and even posted a video explaining its mission and progress. Sadly, after September's landing, Rosetta has ceased its activity on the social networking platform.

## LIGHTING THE WAY
Glow-in-the-dark paths

Polish company TPA Instytut Badań Technicznych made the news in 2016 for their beautiful and innovative bike paths in northern Poland. The paths, made using phosphor, are charged by the sun during the daytime and light up at night to make them safe and visible to cyclists. The paths were apparently inspired by a similar design in the town of Nuenen, in the Netherlands, but the Dutch design utilizes LED technology rather than solar power to light the way.

## SULLY ON SCREEN
### Hudson River heroics

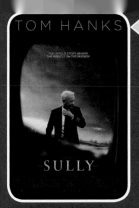

In 2016, Tom Hanks starred as heroic airline pilot Chesley Sullenberger in the biopic *Sully*, directed by Clint Eastwood. The movie tells the true story of Sullenberger's actions in 2009, when he crash-landed his failing plane, US Airways Flight 1549, in New York's Hudson River, saving 155 lives. Fans of the film took to Twitter with a hashtag referencing Sullenberger's impressive feat: #TheMiracleOnTheHudson.

## ALONE IN THE UNIVERSE?
### Newest discovery

In 2016, astronomers at the European Southern Observatory in La Silla, Chile, discovered a planet known as Proxima b orbiting the red dwarf star Proxima Centauri, the nearest star to Earth after the sun. Proxima b, which is 1.3 times the size of Earth, set the science community abuzz because it is in the dwarf star's habitable zone, meaning that its surface temperatures are mild enough for liquid water to collect. Theoretically, this means that Proxima b could support life!

## GOING PLACES
### Most expensive train station

The World Trade Center Transportation Hub, close to the site of the September 11 terror attacks, opened in 2016 after twelve years of construction. Designed by Santiago Calatrava, and reportedly designed in the image of a dove being released by a child, the station cost four billion dollars in public money to build.

# WORLD'S first MONSTER SCHOOL BUS

## BAD TO THE BONE

"Bad to the Bone" is the first monster school bus in the world. This revamped 1956 yellow bus is 13 feet high, thanks to massive tires with 25-inch rims. The oversized bus weighs 19,000 pounds and is a favorite ride at charity events in California. But don't expect to get anywhere in a hurry—this "Kool Bus" is not built for speed and goes at a maximum of just 7 miles per hour.

# MOST EXPENSIVE street-legal car
## KOENIGSEGG CCXR TREVITA

Costing $4.8 million, the Koenigsegg CCXR Trevita is one of the world's most exclusive cars. Koenigsegg, a Swedish manufacturer, built just two Trevitas. One of the vehicle's unique features is the specially created silvery-white, carbon-weave bodywork. In bright light, the finish looks as if it contains millions of tiny white diamonds. It also gives the car its name: Trevita means "three whites" in Swedish. At top speed, the hypercar can hit 254 miles per hour, and it can reach 62 miles per hour in under three seconds.

## MOST EXPENSIVE CARS
(as of 2016) In U.S. dollars

$$$$

**Koenigsegg CCXR Trevita**
$4.8 million

$$$$

**Lamborghini Veneno**
$4.5 million

$$$

**Mansory Vivere Bugatti Veyron** $3.4 million

$$$$

**W Motors Lykan HyperSport**
$3.4 million

$$$

**Ferrari Pininfarina Sergio** $3.0 million

# BIGGEST
# monster truck
# BIGFOOT

Standing 15 feet 6 inches tall and weighing 38,000 pounds, Bigfoot #5 is the king of monster trucks. Bob Chandler purchased a Ford pickup truck in 1974 and began creating the first Bigfoot monster truck in 1975. In 1986, Chandler introduced

Bigfoot #5, the largest ever. The truck's tires are 10 feet tall and come from an Alaskan land train used by the U.S. Army in the 1950s. Chandler built over a dozen more Bigfoot trucks, but none of these newbies matches the size of Bigfoot #5.

# SMALLEST trailer
# QTVAN

The tiny QTvan is just over 7 feet long, 2.5 feet wide, and 5 feet high. Inside, however, it has a full-size single bed, a kettle for boiling water, and a 19-inch TV. The Environmental Transport Association (ETA) in Britain sponsored the invention of the minitrailer, which was designed to be pulled by a mobility scooter. The ETA recommends the QTvan for short trips only, since mobility scooters have a top speed of 6 miles per hour, at best.

59

FASTEST land vehicle

# THRUST SSC

The world's fastest car is the Thrust SSC, which reached a speed of 763 miles per hour on October 15, 1997, in the Black Rock Desert, Nevada. SSC stands for supersonic (faster than the speed of sound). The Thrust SSC's amazing speed comes from two jet engines with 110,000 brake horsepower. That's as much as 145 Formula One race cars. The British-made car uses about 5 gallons of jet fuel in one second and takes just five seconds to reach its top speed. At that speed, the Thrust SSC could travel from New York City to San Francisco in less than four hours. More recently, another British manufacturer has developed a new supersonic car, the Bloodhound, with a projected speed of 1,000 miles per hour. If it reaches that, it will set a new world record.

# FASTEST
# passenger train
# MAGLEV

In April 2015, a Japanese seven-car Maglev train hit a top speed of 375 miles per hour on a test track near Mount Fuji. Maglev trains hover about 4 inches over the tracks. Electrically charged magnets propel the train forward, and it is the lack of friction that enables the train to go at such astonishing speeds. A new track under construction will carry the train 178 miles between Tokyo, Nagoya, and Osaka, cutting travel time by 50 percent. Central Japan Railway expects the train's operational speed to be a maximum of 314 miles per hour.

## FASTEST PASSENGER TRAINS

**Japan Maglev train
375 mph**

**China CRH380AL 302 mph**

**Germany TR-09 279 mph**

**Japan Shinkansen bullet train 275 mph**

**Shanghai Maglev 268 mph**

# on the move

## FASTEST street-legal motorcycle
# MADMAX STREETFIGHTER

The Madmax Streetfighter is the world's fastest street-legal motorcycle with a top speed of 233 miles per hour. A lightweight, high-performance engine with over 500 brake horsepower enables the bike to cover 340 feet per second at full throttle. Maxicorp Autosports Madmax Race Team used the MTT Y2K Turbine Superbike as a basis for its new bike. They made engine parts using strong, but light, titanium and reduced the two-speed gearbox to a single-speed gearbox. However, the Madmax Streetfighter may not be for everyone. It costs over $300,000 to build, and its creators believe it is too powerful for most riders.

# LARGEST cruise ship ROYAL CARIBBEAN
## Harmony of the Seas

With a gross tonnage of 226,963 tons, the new Royal Caribbean cruise ship *Harmony of the Seas* now holds the record for the world's largest. It beats the previous award winners, *Oasis of the Seas* and *Allure of the Seas*, which were also Royal Caribbean ships. The three ships form the company's Oasis Class fleet, with a fourth ship due to launch in 2018. *Harmony of the Seas* carries 6,780 guests. It sets the record for the most slides at sea, and boasts the tallest slide at sea, the Ultimate Abyss, which has a ten-story drop. The ship took her maiden voyage in May 2016.

## WORLD'S LARGEST CRUISE SHIPS
Weight in gross tonnage

*Harmony of the Seas*, **Royal Caribbean**
**226,963**

*Allure of the Seas*,
**Royal Caribbean**
**225,282**

*Oasis of the Seas*,
**Royal Caribbean**
**225,282**

*Quantum of the Seas*,
**Royal Caribbean**
**168,666**

*Anthem of the Seas*,
**Royal Caribbean**
**168,666**

# FASTEST
# helicopter circumnavigation of Earth

## JENNIFER MURRAY AND COLIN BODILL

In 2007, British pilots Jennifer Murray and Colin Bodill became the first pilots ever to fly around the world in a helicopter via the North and South Poles. They also set the record for the fastest time to complete this journey, at 170 days, 22 hours, 47 minutes, and 17 seconds. The pair began and ended their record-setting journey in Fort Worth, Texas, and flew a Bell 407 helicopter. The journey, which began on December 5, 2006, and ended on May 23, 2007, was the duo's second attempt at the record. The first, in 2003, ended with an emergency rescue after they crashed in Antarctica.

# LIGHTEST jet BD-5J MICROJET

In 2004, the BD-5J Microjet, a one-seater aircraft, secured the record as the world's lightest jet. The jet weighs 358.8 pounds, has a 17-foot wingspan, and is just 12 feet long. Engineer Jim Bede introduced the microjet in the early 1970s and sold hundreds in kit form, ready for self-assembly. The BD-5J model became a popular airshow attraction and was featured in a James Bond movie. The microjet uses a TRS-18 turbojet engine and can carry only 32 gallons of fuel. Its top speed is 300 miles per hour.

# FASTEST unmanned plane X-43A

In November 2004, NASA launched its experimental X-43A plane for a test flight over the Pacific Ocean. The X-43A plane reached Mach 9.6, which is more than nine times the speed of sound and nearly 7,000 miles per hour. A B-52B aircraft carried the X-43A and a Pegasus rocket booster into the air, releasing them at 40,000 feet. At that point, the booster—essentially a fuel-packed engine—ignited, blasting the unmanned X-43A higher and faster, before separating from the plane. The plane continued to fly for several minutes at 110,000 feet, before crashing (intentionally) into the ocean.

# man-made objects

## HELIOS 1 AND HELIOS 2

Helios 1 and Helios 2 are space probes launched in the 1970s to orbit the sun. A probe, equipped with cameras, sensors, and computers, can transmit information back to Earth. Both probes are extremely fast, with Helios 2 reaching 153,800 miles per hour. Helios 2 flew closest to the sun, getting within 32 million miles from the center of the enormous star. It takes the probes about 190 days to orbit the sun. In 2018, NASA plans to send another probe, Solar Probe Plus, which will go even closer to the sun. This probe could hit speeds as high as 450,000 miles per hour.

# APOLLO 10 FLIGHT STATS

## 05/18/69
LAUNCH DATE: May 18, 1969

## 12:49
LAUNCH TIME: 12:49 p.m. EDT

## 05/21/69
LUNAR ORBIT: May 21, 1969

## 192:03:23
DURATION OF MISSION: 192 hours, 3 minutes, 23 seconds

## 05/26/69
RETURN DATE: May 26, 1969

## 12:52
SPLASHDOWN: 12:52 p.m. EDT

# FASTEST
# manned
# spacecraft

# APOLLO 10

NASA's *Apollo 10* spacecraft reached its top speed on its descent to Earth, hurtling through the atmosphere at 24,816 miles per hour and splashing down on May 26, 1969. The spacecraft's crew had traveled faster than anyone on Earth. The mission was a "dress rehearsal" for the first moon landing by *Apollo 11*, two months later. The *Apollo 10* spacecraft consisted of a Command Service Module, called Charlie Brown, and a Lunar Module, called Snoopy. Today, Charlie Brown is on display at the Science Museum in London, England.

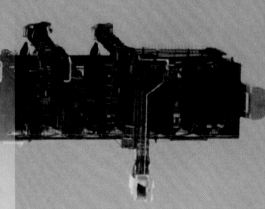

**LIFT-OFF**
The *Apollo 10* spacecraft was launched from Cape Canaveral, known at the time, as Cape Kennedy at the time. It was the fourth manned Apollo launch in seven months.

# FASTEST
# roller coaster
# FORMULA ROSSA

## FASTEST ROLLER COASTERS

**Formula Rossa, Abu Dhabi, UAE 149.1 mph**

**Kingda Ka, New Jersey, USA 128 mph**

**Top Thrill Dragster, Ohio, USA 120 mph**

**Dodonpa, Yamanashi, Japan 107 mph**

**Tower of Terror II, Queensland, Australia 100 mph**

**FORMULA ROSSA**
World Records
**Speed: 149.1 mph**
**G-FORCE: 1.7 Gs**
**Acceleration: 4.8 Gs**

Thrill seekers hurtle along the Formula Rossa track at 149.1 miles per hour. The high-speed roller coaster is part of Ferrari World in Abu Dhabi, United Arab Emirates. At 925,696 square miles, Ferrari World is the world's largest indoor theme park. The Formula Rossa roller coaster seats are red Ferrari-shaped cars that travel from 0 to 62 miles per hour in just two seconds—as fast as a race car. The ride's G-Force is so extreme that passengers must wear goggles to protect their eyes. G-Force acts on a body due to acceleration and gravity. People can withstand 6 to 8 Gs for short periods. The Formula Rossa G-Force is 4.8 Gs during acceleration and 1.7 Gs at maximum speed.

# TALLEST water coaster

# MASSIV

Schlitterbahn Galveston Island Waterpark in Texas is home to the world's tallest water coaster—the aptly named MASSIV, which measured in at 81 feet and 6.72 inches tall in June 2016. A water coaster is a water slide that features ascents as well as descents, with riders traveling in rafts or tubes. MASSIV, which the park calls a "monster blaster," was built for the tenth anniversary of the opening of Schlitterbahn Galveston. Riders sit in two-person tubes, which take them over a series of dips and four uphill climbs before dropping into the final landing pool. In April 2016, the park released a virtual version of the ride, allowing people all over the world to see MASSIV from the point of view of a rider.

CIRCUS

OLDEST
# merry-go-round
# FLYING HORSES CAROUSEL

Taking a spin around the Flying Horses Carousel in Martha's Vineyard is a trip back in time. Charles Dare constructed the carousel in 1876 for an amusement park in Coney Island, New York. The carousel moved to Oak Bluffs, Massachusetts, in 1884. A preservation society took over Flying Horses in 1986 to restore the carousel and keep it intact and working. Today, the horses look just as colorful as they did in the 1800s. Their manes are real horsehair and they have glass eyes. As the horses turn around and around, a 1923 Wurlitzer Band Organ plays old-time music. The Flying Horses Carousel is a National Landmark.

# LARGEST tunnel-boring machine

# BERTHA

In July 2013, Bertha started drilling out a 2-mile-long tunnel beneath Seattle, Washington. Bertha is a tunnel-boring machine built in Japan at a cost of $80 million. She weighs 7,000 tons and, at 300 feet long, she is almost the length of a football field. The machine's massive cutting head alone is 57.5 feet in diameter and consists of a steel face and 600 cutting disks. In December 2013, Bertha stopped working. The crew dug an access pit to retrieve her cutting head for repairs. In December 2015, Bertha resumed her work. The machine's fans follow Bertha's progress on her Twitter page. At one point she had 72,000 followers.

**4**

# STRUCTURES

**super**

# SUPER STRUCTURES
# TRENDING#

## SOCIAL CENTRAL
### #EiffelTower

Paris was the world's third most Instagrammed city of 2016, but number one for pictures of couples—ahead of Milan, Madrid, and Venice. The Eiffel Tower once again won the title of the world's most Instagrammed building, beating out the nearby Louvre Museum, Rome's Colosseum, and New York City's Empire State Building. Paris's famous tower looked noticeably different in June thanks to the Euro 2016 soccer tournament; each day of the tournament, the tower was lit up in the colors of the team whose fans were most active on social media that day.

## ARCHITECTURAL FAIL
### Britain's ugliest building

The 2016 Carbuncle Cup, an award for Britain's ugliest building, was given to Lincoln Plaza, a new residential block in London's Docklands. *Building Design*, the magazine behind the award, called the thirty-one-story apartment complex a "brain-numbing jumble of discordant shapes, patterns, materials, and colors." 2016 marked the fifth year in a row that a London building has won the unflattering title.

## UNDERGROUND OBSESSION
### Elite disaster preparation

2016 saw a new trend in real estate, with companies reporting a 700% rise in commissions of underground bunkers by the global elite. Costing millions of dollars to build, these lavish complexes come complete with high-tech amenities, swimming pools, and even bowling alleys. They provide their owners with safe and comfortable long-term shelters in the event of a major catastrophe.

## CHINA SAYS NO!
### A ban on wacky new builds

China officially banned flamboyant architecture in 2016; its State Council and the Communist Party's Central Committee declared in February that "oversized, xenocentric, weird" designs would no longer be approved for construction. This edict brings an end to a run of strange structures going up in the country—like the teapot-shaped Wuxi Wanda Cultural Tourism City Exhibition Center, which opened in 2014.

## RIVER CROSSING
### Most Instagrammed bridge

The Brooklyn Bridge in New York City was the world's most Instagrammed bridge in 2016, ahead of last year's winner, the Golden Gate Bridge in San Francisco. The Brooklyn Bridge, which connects the New York boroughs of Brooklyn and Manhattan, opened in 1883. According to the city's department of transportation, it is now crossed each day by 120,000 vehicles, 4,000 pedestrians, and 3,100 bicyclists.

CITY WITH THE MOST
# skyscrapers in the world
# HONG KONG

Hong Kong, China, has 316 buildings that reach 500 feet or higher, and three more under construction. Six are 980 feet or higher. The tallest three are the International Commerce Centre (ICC) at 1,588 feet; Two International Finance Centre at 1,352 feet; and Central Plaza at 1,227 feet. Hong Kong's stunning skyline towers above Victoria Harbour. Most of its tallest buildings are on Hong Kong Island, although the other side of the harbor, Kowloon, is growing. Every night a light, laser, and sound show called "A Symphony of Lights" illuminates the sky against a backdrop of some forty of Hong Kong's skyscrapers.

## CITIES WITH THE MOST SKYSCRAPERS IN THE WORLD
Number of skyscrapers at 500 feet or higher

Hong Kong, China 316

New York City, USA 251

Dubai, UAE 156

Shanghai, China 133

# LARGEST
## sports stadium
# RUNGRADO MAY FIRST STADIUM

It took over two years to build Rungrado May First Stadium, a gigantic sports venue that seats up to 150,000 people. The 197-foot-high stadium opened in 1989 on Rungra Island in North Korea's capital, Pyongyang. The stadium hosts international soccer matches on its natural grass pitch, and has other facilities such as an indoor swimming pool, training halls, and a 1,312-foot rubberized running track. The annual gymnastics and artistic festival Arirang also takes place here.

## LARGEST SPORTS STADIUMS
By capacity

**Rungrado May First Stadium, North Korea 150,000**

**Michigan Stadium, Michigan, USA 107,601**

**Beaver Stadium, Pennsylvania, USA 107, 282**

**Estadio Azteca, Mexico 105, 064**

**AT&T Stadium, Texas, USA 105,000**

# LARGEST home in an airliner 727 BOEING

Bruce Campbell's home is not that large, but it is the biggest of its kind. Campbell lives in 1,066 square feet within a grounded 727 Boeing airplane. The airplane no longer has an engine, but Campbell kept the cockpit and its original instruments. He also installed a transparent floor to make the structure of the plane visible. The retired engineer purchased the plane for $100,000 and paid for its transportation to his property in Oregon. Now trees surround the plane instead of sky. Visitors are welcome to take a tour.

# LARGEST
# house shaped like a vw beetle
# VOGLREITER RESIDENCE

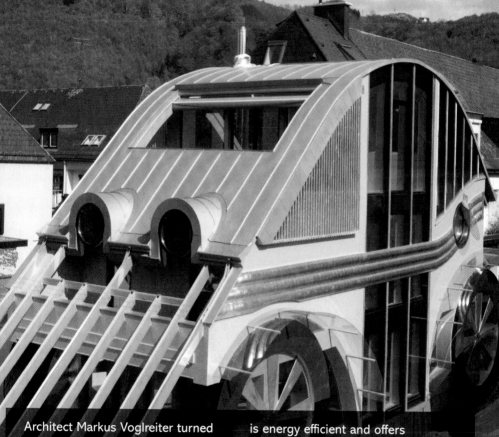

Architect Markus Voglreiter turned an ordinary home in Gnigl, near Salzburg, Austria, into an attention-grabbing showpiece: a Volkswagen Beetle–shaped house. The eco-friendly home, completed in 2003, is energy efficient and offers separate, comfortable living quarters. The car-shaped extension measures 950 square feet and is over 32 feet high. At night, two of the home's windows look like car headlights.

# WORLD'S MOST
## expensive hotel
# THE MARK, NY, USA

In September 2015, New York's Mark Hotel unveiled the world's most expensive suite: a penthouse with a price tag starting at $75,000 per night. At 12,000 square feet, the Mark penthouse is 6,000 square feet smaller than the next most expensive, at the Hotel President Wilson in Geneva, Switzerland. The Mark occupies a prime piece of real estate on Manhattan's Upper East Side, and the suite's terrace boasts views over Central Park and the Metropolitan Museum of Art. Spanning two floors, the penthouse has a private elevator and library. It is ideal for hosting events, with 26-foot-high ceilings in the living room—which doubles as a grand ballroom—and a dining table that seats twenty-four guests.

# hotel made of salt
# PALACIO DE SAL

Hotel Palacio de Sal in Uyuni, Bolivia, is the first hotel in the world made completely out of salt. Originally built in 1998, construction began on the new Palacio de Sal hotel in 2004. The hotel overlooks the biggest salt flat in the world, Salar de Uyuni, which covers 4,086 square miles. Builders used around one million blocks of salt to create the hotel walls, floors, ceilings, and furniture. Some of the hotel's thirty rooms have igloo-shaped roofs. The salt flats lie in an area once covered by Lago Minchin, an ancient salt lake. When the lake dried up, it left salt pans, one of which was the Salar de Uyuni.

## ANOTHER STRANGE PLACE TO STAY
Hotel shaped like a dog: Dog Bark Park Inn in Cottonwood, Idaho, where you can sleep inside a wooden beagle that measures 33 feet high and 16 feet wide.

83

# DUBAI'S BURJ KHALIFA
## WORLD RECORDS:

Most floors: 160

Fastest elevators: 55 feet per second

Highest vertical concrete pumping: 1,972 feet

Laid end to end the steel used here would stretch one-quarter of the way around the world!

WORLD'S TALLEST

building

# BURJ KHALIFA

IT CAN SWAY UP TO 3.9 FEET!

## GOING UP!

THE UPPER SECTION IS STEEL FRAMED, SO IT'S POSSIBLE TO MAKE IT TALLER. DURING BUILDING, ITS HEIGHT WAS RAISED THREE TIMES.

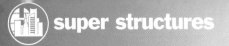

# LARGEST freestanding building

# NEW CENTURY GLOBAL CENTER

The New Century Global Center in Chengdu, southwestern China, is an enormous 18.9 million square feet. That's nearly three times the size of the U.S. Pentagon. Completed in 2013, the structure is 328 feet high, 1,640 feet long, and 1,312 feet deep. The multiuse building houses a 4.3-million-square-foot shopping mall, two hotels, an Olympic-size ice rink, a fourteen-screen IMAX cinema complex, and offices. It even has its own Paradise Island, a beach resort complete with artificial sun.

# swimming pool LARGEST
# CITYSTARS
# POOL

The Citystars lagoon in Sharm el-Sheikh, Egypt, stretches over 30 acres. It was created by Crystal Lagoons, the same company that built the former record holder at San Alfonso del Mar in Chile. The lagoon at Sharm el-Sheikh cost $5.5 million to create and is designed to be sustainable, using salt water from local underground aquifers. The creators purify this water not just for recreation, but also to provide clean, fresh water to the surrounding community.

## LARGEST SWIMMING POOLS
Size in acres

Citystars, Egypt 30.0

San Alfonso del Mar, Chile 19.7

Ocean Dome, Japan 7.4

Dead Sea, China 7.4

Orthlieb Pool, Morocco 3.7

TALLEST
# tree house
# THE MINISTER'S HOUSE

Minister Horace Burgess began building his tree house in 1993, and took many years erecting the towering, ten-story, 97-foot-high structure. The main support is an 80-foot-tall white oak tree, while six other trees provide reinforcement. The Minister's House, as it is known, is in a wooded area in Crossville, Tennessee, and includes a church topped by a chime tower. Thousands came to visit the amazing attraction every year, until the State Fire Marshal temporarily closed the tree house in 2012 due to fire hazards.

# WORLD'S
## greenest city
# REYKJAVIK

According to conservation organization Frontier, Iceland's capital city continues to be the world's greenest. Reykjavik gets nearly 100 percent of its electricity from geothermal and hydrogen power and more than 80 percent of its primary energy—heating and transportation—from renewable sources. The city began its green movement in the early 1900s when farmers began using natural hot springs to heat their homes. Reykjavik aims to be completely fossil-fuel-free by 2050, and is close to reaching that goal, as fossil fuels generate just 0.1% of the city's energy. Its transportation system is also one of the world's greenest. Its buses currently run on zero-emission hydrogen power.

## GREENEST CITIES 2016
according to Frontier

♻♻♻♻♻ Reykjavik, Iceland

♻♻♻♻ Curitiba, Brazil

♻♻♻ Freiburg, Germany

♻♻ Copenhagen, Denmark

♻ Oslo, Norway

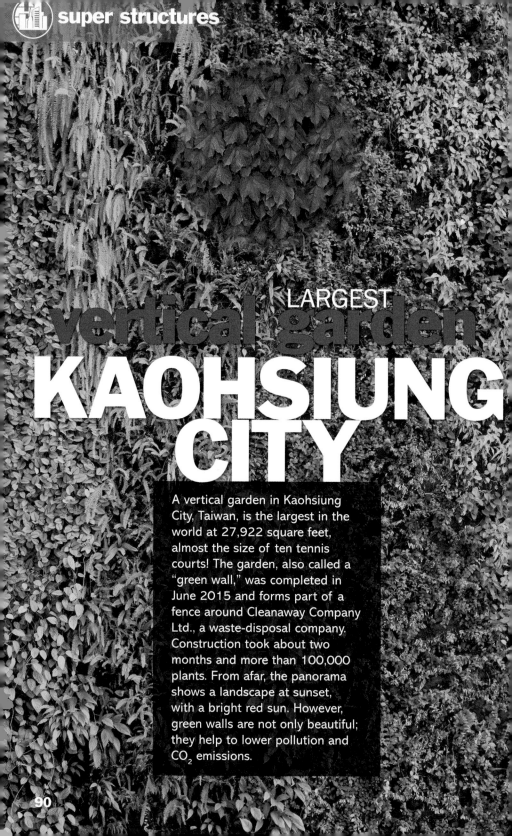

# LARGEST
# vertical garden
# KAOHSIUNG CITY

A vertical garden in Kaohsiung City, Taiwan, is the largest in the world at 27,922 square feet, almost the size of ten tennis courts! The garden, also called a "green wall," was completed in June 2015 and forms part of a fence around Cleanaway Company Ltd., a waste-disposal company. Construction took about two months and more than 100,000 plants. From afar, the panorama shows a landscape at sunset, with a bright red sun. However, green walls are not only beautiful; they help to lower pollution and $CO_2$ emissions.

# WORLD'S LARGEST greenhouse EDEN PROJECT

## COUNTRY WITH THE MOST GREENHOUSES

The Netherlands: Greenhouses cover more than 25 square miles of the country's entire area.

The Eden Project sprawls over 32 acres of land in the countryside of Cornwall, England. Nestled in the cavity of an old clay pit mine, it's the world's largest greenhouse and has been open since 2003. Eight interlinked, transparent domes house two distinct biomes. The first is a rain-forest region and the second is Mediterranean. Each has around one thousand plant varieties. Visitors can see a further three thousand different plants in the 20 acres of outdoor gardens. During construction, the Eden Project used a record-breaking 230 miles of scaffolding.

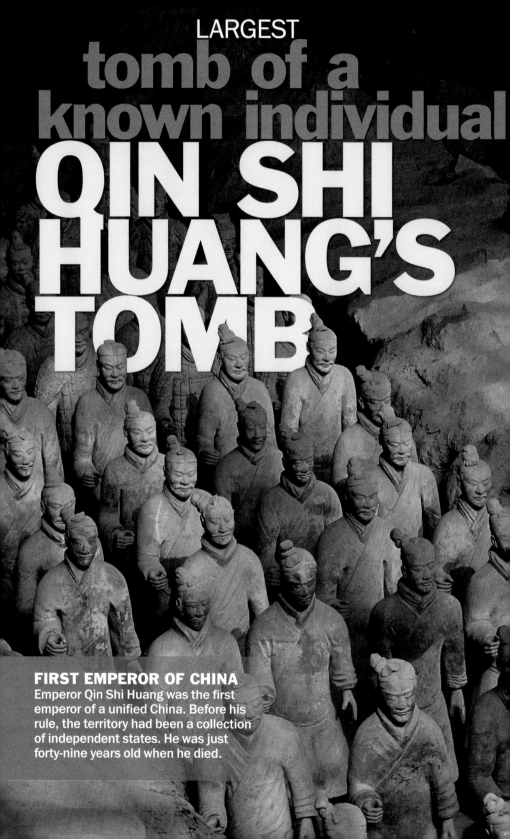

# LARGEST tomb of a known individual

# QIN SHI HUANG'S TOMB

**FIRST EMPEROR OF CHINA**
Emperor Qin Shi Huang was the first emperor of a unified China. Before his rule, the territory had been a collection of independent states. He was just forty-nine years old when he died.

# QIN SHI HUANG'S TOMB STATS

## 1974
YEAR OF DISCOVERY: 1974

## 36
NUMBER OF YEARS IT TOOK TO CREATE: 36

## 8,000
TOTAL NUMBER OF FIGURES FOUND: 8,000

## 221–207
DURATION OF THE QIN DYNASTY: 221–207 B.C.E.

Emperor Qin Shi Huang ruled China from 221 B.C.E. to 207 B.C.E. He is famous for uniting China's empire. In 1974, people digging a well in the fields northeast of Xi'an, in Shaanxi province, accidentally discovered the ancient tomb. Further investigation by archaeologists revealed a burial complex over 20 square miles. A large pit contained 6,000 life-size terra-cotta warrior figures, each one different from the next and dressed according to rank. A second and third pit contained 2,000 more figures, clay horses, some 40,000 bronze weapons, and other artifacts. Historians think that 700,000 people worked for about thirty-six years to create this incredible mausoleum. The emperor's tomb remains sealed to preserve its contents and to protect workers from possible hazards, such as chemical poisoning from mercury in the surrounding soil.

LARGEST
## castle
# PRAGUE CASTLE

Founded in the late ninth century, Prague Castle is officially the largest coherent castle complex in the world. Covering 750,000 square feet, the castle grounds span enough land for seven football fields, with buildings in various architectural styles that have been added and renovated throughout the centuries. Formerly the home of kings and empresses, the castle is now occupied by the president of the Czech Republic and his family, and is also open to tourists. The palace contains four churches, including the famous St. Vitus Cathedral.

# LARGEST
# sand
# castle
# VIRGINIA
# KEY BEACH

It took ninety-two hours in all for a team of twenty people to create the world's tallest sand castle at Virginia Key Beach, near Miami, Florida, in October 2015. At 45 feet, 10¼ inches, it is taller than a four-story building. The crew used 1,800 tons of sand to sculpt the castle, which features sculptures of India's Taj Mahal and Italy's Leaning Tower of Pisa, among other landmarks. Turkish Airlines commissioned the sand castle to celebrate a new flight route from Miami to Istanbul, Turkey.

# RECORD-BREAKING
## LEGO® structure
# LEGOLAND®
# GÜNZBERG

Between June 24 and June 30, 2016, builders at LEGOLAND® Deutschland, in Günzberg, Germany, beat the previous record set in Milan to create the world's tallest LEGO® tower. Measuring 116 feet and 4 inches, the tower took nearly 600,000 bricks to complete. Both the Günzberg and Milan structures were simple towers, but in 2016, a new record was also set for the world's tallest LEGO® building—a replica of Burj Khalifa at LEGOLAND® Dubai.

# LARGEST
## sculpture cut from a single piece of stone
# SPHINX

The Great Sphinx stands guard near three large pyramids at Giza, Egypt. Historians believe that ancient people created the gigantic sculpture about 4,500 years ago for the pharaoh Khafre. They carved the sphinx from one mass of limestone in the desert floor, creating a sculpture about 66 feet high and 240 feet long. It has the head of a pharaoh and the body of a lion. The sculpture may represent Ruti, a twin lion god from ancient myths that protected the sun god, Ra, and guarded entrances to the underworld. Sand has covered and preserved the Great Sphinx, but over many years, wind and humidity have worn parts of the soft limestone away, for example, on the sphinx's head and back.

**GREAT SPHINX
WORLD RECORDS**
Age: 4,500 years (estimated)
Length: 240 ft
Height: 66 ft

**5**

high
TECH

# HIGH TECH
# TRENDING #

## RIP VINE
### Video app shuts down

The founders of short video app Vine officially announced its discontinuation in October 2016, prompting a rash of #RIPVine memes across social media as people reshared their favorite posts. Vine, which allowed users to upload six-second clips, created its own crop of celebrities, many of them teens like Cameron Dallas and Nash Grier. The app's death also heralded the end of a vlogger rallying cry: "Do it for the vine."

## APRIL FOOLS!
### Joke backfires on Google

Tech giant Google celebrated April Fools' Day 2016 by replacing the "send and archive" button in Gmail with "send with mic drop"—attaching a funny GIF of a *Despicable Me* minion to the end of the message before sending. Unfortunately, not all of their customers were laughing at the joke, and Google was forced to end the feature early and apologize after angry users reported accidentally sending the GIF in serious or business conversations.

## SNAP HAPPY
### Most downloaded app of 2016

Instant photo-sharing app Snapchat was 2016's most downloaded free app, according to Apple's App Store, replacing Trivia Crack in the number one spot. 2016 was a big year for Snapchat, seeing its release of several new filters and stickers, and also Spectacles: glasses that users can wear to take first-person-style images and videos of the world around them.

## EMBARRASSING PARENTS
### "Chewbacca Mom" goes viral

Candace Payne's hilarious viral video was the most watched Facebook Live clip of 2016, with 162 million views. The video—which shows Payne in her car putting on a Chewbacca mask she bought at Kohl's and then laughing hysterically—made the mother of two instantly famous, while the Kohl's website immediately sold out of the featured mask.

## THE FUTURE OF TECH
### AlphaGo takes the prize

When AlphaGo, a computer program created by Google subsidiary DeepMind, defeated the world champion human player Lee Sedol at the game of Go in 2016, it signaled a major victory for advancements in artificial intelligence. Go, an East Asian board game, was previously considered too conceptual—requiring human thought processes such as reaction and intuition—for machines to beat a professional human under regular tournament conditions. The five-game series between Sedol and AlphaGo can be watched in full on DeepMind's YouTube channel.

## CELEBRITY WITH THE MOST Instagram followers
# SELENA GOMEZ

## CELEBRITIES WITH THE MOST INSTAGRAM FOLLOWERS 2016
In millions of followers

- Selena Gomez 103
- Taylor Swift 94.1
- Ariana Grande 90.5
- Beyoncé 89.4
- Kim Kardashian West 88.5

Singer and former Disney Channel star Selena Gomez reached 103 million Instagram followers in 2016, eclipsing her BFF Taylor Swift as the most popular celebrity Instagrammer. Gomez also had the top five most liked Instagram photographs of 2016, with the most popular shot showing Gomez drinking a Coke with her own lyrics on the bottle. The photo, which has more than 6.3 million likes so far, stole the title of most liked Instagram photo ever from Gomez's own ex-boyfriend, Justin Bieber.

## MOST RETWEETED
# photo ever
# ELLEN DEGENERES

Ellen DeGeneres's selfie taken at the 2014 Oscars is the most retweeted photo ever. The photo, which pictures DeGeneres, Bradley Cooper, Jennifer Lawrence, and many other celebrities, has over 3.3 million retweets. In just over one hour, the post was retweeted over 1 million times. The rush of activity on Twitter crashed the social networking site for a short time. Before the Oscar selfie took over Twitter, President Obama held the record for the most retweeted photo. On November 6, 2012, the president posted an election victory photo and tweet that has been retweeted over 800,000 times.

# CLASH OF CLANS

## TOP-GROSSING mobile game app

Five years after its initial release in 2012, the free online gaming app *Clash of Clans* currently has the highest daily revenue of all iPhone gaming apps. Gamers develop clan bases, which they must defend against invading forces. It's as simple as that! However, the action continues when players leave the game, which means they have to check in to make sure their clan is not under attack. Gaming critics and fans believe this is a major factor in the game's success.

## TOP-GROSSING MOBILE GAME APPS
Daily revenue in U.S. dollars
(as of April 2017)

**Clash of Clans**
1,975,223

**Clash Royale**
1,480,799

**Candy Crush Saga**
1,135,624

**Mobile Strike**
578,288

**Game of War:
Fire Age**
384,772

# MOST VIEWED
# YouTube video ever
# "GANGNAM STYLE"

Since South Korean singer Psy released "Gangnam Style" in July 2012, views of his video on YouTube have soared to over 2.4 billion. The music video had more than 500,000 views on its first day and became the first video to reach one billion. Google, which owns YouTube, had to upgrade the data processing system when "Gangnam Style" pushed the YouTube viewing counter past its limit of 2.14 billion. In 2013, Psy's follow-up, "Gentleman," gained over 900 million views.

# MOST-USED
# Instagram
# hashtag

The most popular hashtag on Instagram in 2016 was used to caption a variety of photographs—romantic selfies, family photos, even shots of new shoes. The picture-sharing platform displays more than 960 million posts that use the tag #love, and the number continues to grow. It comes as no surprise that the most popular emoji on Instagram in 2016 was the red heart, while four of the remaining top ten emojis contained a heart as well.

# ZOELLA

## MOST INFLUENTIAL
# beauty vlogger

British vlogger Zoe "Zoella" Sugg was named 2016's top beauty influencer by video technology company Zefr. The ranking system takes into account not just the number of followers each account has but also the number of views and engagements it gets—that is, the number of shares, comments, and likes. Zoella had 252 million engagements in 2016 alone, and 30 million followers across her social media platforms. Zoella has translated her influencer status into real money, with her own line of beauty products and a reported income of over $71,000 a month from her YouTube channel alone.

## TOP BEAUTY VLOGGERS 2016
Number of engagements in millions

**Zoella 252**

**Niki and Gabi Demartino 211**

**Jaclyn Hill 114**

**Shaaanxo 105**

**Carli Bybel 103**

# PRODUCT WITH THE MOST
# Facebook fans
# COCA-COLA

Soft drink giant Coca-Cola was again the most popular product on Facebook in 2016 with 102.8 million fans. The company posts photographs, videos, and updates on its Timeline while fans can post their own photos and questions for the company. Founded in 1886, Coca-Cola is now a multibillion-dollar enterprise, producing 3,500 different types of beverages, including Dasani, Evian, and Minute Maid. The drinks sell in over 200 countries worldwide at a staggering rate of 1.9 billion servings per day.

## PRODUCTS WITH THE MOST FACEBOOK FANS
In millions of fans, as of February 2017

     **Coca-Cola 102.8**

    **Red Bull 47.1**

   **Oreo 42.6**

 **Nike Football 42.5**

 **Converse 37.2**

# PERSON WITH THE MOST
# Facebook "likes"

Soccer pro Cristiano Ronaldo retained the top spot on Facebook in 2016 with over 108 million fans. Born in 1985, Ronaldo plays for both the Portuguese national team and Spanish powerhouse Real Madrid. As a teenager, Ronaldo's soccer skills were so impressive that British team Manchester United signed him for around $17 million. In 2008, Ronaldo earned the honor of FIFA World Player of the Year. The following year, Ronaldo transferred to Real Madrid for a record $115 million. Among his many awards is the European Golden Shoe, which Ronaldo has won a record four times.

## PEOPLE WITH THE MOST FACEBOOK FANS

In millions of fans, as of February 2017

    **Cristiano Ronaldo 119.57**

   **Shakira 104.49**

   **Vin Diesel 101.22**

 **Eminem 90.94**

 **Lionel Messi 87.91**

# CRISTIANO
# RONALDO

## DOG WITH THE MOST

## Instagram followers

# MARU TARO

Maru, a Shiba Inu living in Japan, is the most popular dog on Instagram, with 2.5 million followers. Maru belongs to Shinjiro Ono, a forty-two-year-old business owner in Tokyo, who began posting daily pictures of Maru's squinty-eyed grin and adorable antics in 2011. Shinjiro Ono simply wanted to spread some joy in the wake of the Great East Japan Earthquake. Maru is now the star of three photo books produced by Kadokawa Corporation.

# CAT WITH THE MOST Instagram followers
## TARDAR SAUCE
## (GRUMPY CAT)

Tardar Sauce, more commonly known as Grumpy Cat, just might be the world's most famous feline, boasting 2.1 million followers on Instagram. She is best known for the permanently "grumpy" expression—caused by feline dwarfism and an underbite—that made her famous after her owners, brother and sister Bryan Bundesen and Tabatha Bundesen, shared photographs of her on Reddit in 2012. The Bundesen siblings have parlayed the feline's fame into cash, with Grumpy Cat merchandise and an endorsement deal with Nestlé Purina PetCare. Tardar Sauce was born in the Bundesen family home in Arizona on April 4, 2012, and has a brother named Pokey.

# TOP-EARNING
# gamer
# SAAHIL
# "UNiVeRsE"
# ARORA
# $2,708,036

Saahil Arora, who plays under the handle UNiVeRse, finished 2016 as the highest-earning eSports star, with $2,708,036 in lifetime earnings since 2011. Arora's biggest year was 2015, when he earned $1.7 million at the age of 25. The San Francisco resident played for Team Secret between March and June 2016, when he returned to his former team, the Evil Geniuses. Founded in 1991, Evil Geniuses claims to be the world's most elite gaming team, and has some big-name sponsors, such as Monster Energy drinks. The second-highest earning eSports star, Peter "ppd" Dager, retired at the end of 2016, having earned $2,618,120 in prize money during his career.

# MOST POPULAR
# online game

In 2016, Riot Games reported that *League of Legends* had reached 100 million monthly players—meaning that it now has as many monthly users as Spotify, and more subscribers than Netflix. Riot Games created *League of Legends* in 2009, and it quickly became one of the most popular MOBA—Multiplayer Online Battle Arena— games. The game is free to play, although players purchase points to buy "champions," "boosts," and other virtual items to help them on the battlefield. The game is big among eSports players, with teams competing in the *League of Legends* World Championship contests for big money.

# LEAGUE OF LEGENDS

## MOST POPULAR ONLINE GAMES 2016
Number of unique users (in millions)

 League of Legends 100

 Hearthstone 50

Overwatch 20

DotA 2 15

World of Warcraft 5.5

# -BESTSELLING
# gaming console

Sony's PlayStation 2 game console is the bestselling gaming hardware of all time, with 155 million systems sold between its introduction in 2000 and the cease of production in 2012. Sony's newer consoles are yet to come close to achieving the same numbers—only the original PlayStation, which was produced from 1994 to 2006, managed to pass the 100 million sales threshold. The only other consoles to reach 100 million—coming in a close second to the PlayStation 2—are handheld machines: the Nintendo DS, which sold 154 million units, and Nintendo's Game Boy and Game Boy Color, which combined to sell 154 million units. More than 3,800 PlayStation 2 games were released during the console's lifetime. Many of its most popular games, known as PlayStation Classics, were remastered for play on later consoles, such as cult favorite *Destroy All Humans!*, which was released for PlayStation 4 in 2016.

# PLAYSTATION 2

# BESTSELLING
## video game
## franchise
## of all time
# MARIO

Nintendo's Mario franchise has sold 528.5 million units since the first game was released in 1981. Since then, Mario, his brother Luigi, and other characters like Princess Peach and Yoshi have become household names, starring in a number of games across consoles. In the early games, like *Super Mario World*, players jump over obstacles, collect tokens, and capture flags as Mario journeys through the Mushroom Kingdom to save the princess. The franchise has since diversified to include other popular games, such as *Mario Kart*, a racing game showcasing the inhabitants and landscapes of Mushroom Kingdom.

## BESTSELLING VIDEO GAME FRANCHISES
Units sold in millions

 **Mario (Nintendo)**
**528.5**

 **Tetris (The Tetris Company) 495**

 **Pokémon (Game Freak) 280**

 **Call of Duty (Infinity Ward) 250**

 **Grand Theft Auto (Rockstar North) 240 million**

Minecon 2015, a gathering of *Minecraft* fans, was the biggest convention ever for a single video game. The event, held July 4–5 in London, England, attracted 10,000 people from seventy-three countries. Gaming developer Markus Persson created *Minecraft* in 2009 and sold it to Microsoft in 2014 for $2.5 billion. Gamers can play alone or with other players online. The game involves breaking and placing blocks to build whatever gamers can imagine—from simple constructions to huge virtual worlds. In 2014, the Ordnance Survey (O.S.) of Great Britain created the largest real-world-inspired place in *Minecraft*. Using O.S. geographical data, the creators used eighty-three billion blocks to create a map of the British Isles. At the end of 2015, *Minecraft* had sold over $22 million in PC/Mac games and had over seventy million users worldwide.

MINECRAFT STATS:

# 10,000

NUMBER OF PEOPLE ATTENDING
MINECON 2015: 10,000

# 73

NUMBER OF COUNTRIES
REPRESENTED BY ATTENDEES: 73

# 22

NUMBER OF PC/MAC GAMES SOLD:
OVER $22 million

# 2.5

PRICE MICROSOFT PAID FOR THE
GAME: $2.5 billion

BIGGEST
CONVENTION
for a single
video game
MINECON
2015

# OPPORTUNITY

## rover on mars

### LONGEST-SURVIVING

Since January 2004, the Opportunity rover has been exploring planet Mars. The 384-pound NASA rover left Earth on July 7, 2003, to travel 283 million miles to Mars. Its twin rover, Spirit, left in June. The rovers, equipped with cameras and scientific equipment, landed on opposite sides of Mars and collected data on the planet's surface. NASA expected the mission to last ninety days but decided to keep the rovers on the Red Planet to explore further. NASA lost contact with Spirit in 2011, but Opportunity continues to roam Mars.

# LARGEST single machine

# LARGE HADRON COLLIDER

The Large Hadron Collider (LHC) is a 16-mile, ring-shaped machine that sits 328 feet below ground on the French/Swiss border. In 2008, the European Organization for Nuclear Research (CERN) switched on the machine that thousands of scientists and engineers spent years building. They hope that the gigantic collider will explain many mysteries of the universe by examining its tiniest particles, called hadrons. The machine makes these particles travel almost at the speed of light and records what happens when they collide. The aim is to examine various scientific theories, including the idea that the universe originated in a massive cosmic explosion known as the Big Bang.

Fanny is a massive 26-foot-high, 51-foot-long, fire-breathing dragon. She is also the world's biggest walking robot. In 2012, a German company designed and built Fanny using both hydraulic and electronic parts. She is radio remote-controlled with nine controllers, while 238 sensors allow the robot to assess her environment. She does this while walking on her four legs or stretching wings that span 39 feet. Powered by a 140-horsepower diesel engine, Fanny weighs a hefty 24,250 pounds—as much as two elephants—and breathes real fire using 24 pounds of liquid gas.

# BIGGEST
# walking robot
# FANNY

## FANNY STATS:

# 09/27/2012

DATE OF FANNY'S LAUNCH: **September 27, 2012**

# 26' 10"

FANNY'S HEIGHT: **26 feet, 10 inches**

# 51' 6"

FANNY'S LENGTH: **51 feet, 6 inches**

# 12'

FANNY'S BODY WIDTH: **12 feet**

# 39'

FANNY'S WINGSPAN: **39 feet**

# SMALLEST ROBOBEE robot

The RoboBee is smaller than a paperclip and can fly and dive into water. Scientists and engineers at Harvard University developed the tiny robot, which has a wingspan of just over an inch and can flap its wings 120 times per second. Sensors and electronics make the bee "see" and react to its environment. Its carbon-fiber body weighs a fraction of an ounce.

Initially, the lightweight robot could not break the surface of the water, so its designers lowered the wing speed to just nine beats per second. This enabled the RoboBee to get into the water and swim, but the robot cannot go back to the air. Because the RoboBee is so small, it could be useful in search-and-rescue missions and, possibly, crop pollination.

The Traxxas XO-1 Supercar can hit 100 miles per hour in 4.29 seconds, and reach a top speed of 118 miles per hour. The car is the fastest ready-to-race, radio-controlled car in the world. The Traxxas XO-1 comes ready to go with a brushless motor that generates 3.5 horsepower. It weighs just over 13 pounds and measures 27 inches long and almost 12 inches wide. A link app provides additional control over the radio and includes graphic data showing speed, RPM, and more. This kind of performance doesn't come cheap—even the base model Traxxas XO-1 costs as much as $750.

## FASTEST
## remote-controlled car
# TRAXXAS XO-1
# SUPERCAR

# amazing ANIMALS

# WILD ANIMALS
# TRENDING #

## AMAZING ARACHNIDS
### New spider species is discovered

Harry Potter fans around the world were delighted by the identification of a new species of spider in December 2016. Discovered by scientists and self-professed "geeks" in India's Western Ghats mountain range, the spider looks remarkably like the Sorting Hat from the wizarding series, leading the scientists to name the species Eriovixia gryffindori, after the hat's owner and Hogwarts founder Godric Gryffindor.

## PANDA DIPLOMACY
### Twitter reacts to the cutest ambassadors

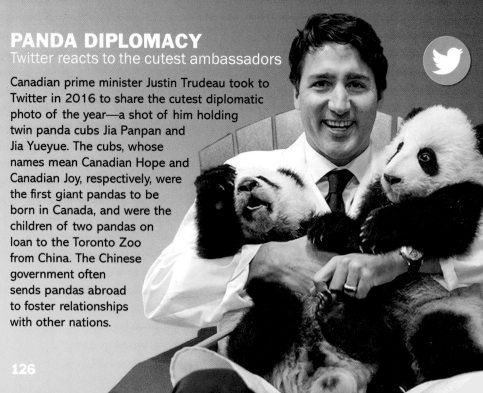

Canadian prime minister Justin Trudeau took to Twitter in 2016 to share the cutest diplomatic photo of the year—a shot of him holding twin panda cubs Jia Panpan and Jia Yueyue. The cubs, whose names mean Canadian Hope and Canadian Joy, respectively, were the first giant pandas to be born in Canada, and were the children of two pandas on loan to the Toronto Zoo from China. The Chinese government often sends pandas abroad to foster relationships with other nations.

# NO MORE SHOWS
## Curtain falls on SeaWorld orca breeding

In March 2016, SeaWorld announced that it will no longer capture and breed killer whales for its famous shows, a move celebrated by many animal rights activists and others. The park made the decision after attendance fell in the wake of the 2013 documentary Blackfish, which shows the danger and cruelty of keeping orcas in captivity. The decision also followed the 2016 announcement that the orca featured in the documentary, Tilikum, was fatally ill. Tilikum passed away in the early days of 2017.

# GREAT ESCAPE
## Inky the octopus escapes

In a scene reminiscent of Pixar's *Finding Nemo*, a common New Zealand octopus named Inky made headlines in April 2016 when he escaped his tank at an aquarium and reportedly slithered down a 164-foot pipe to get back to the ocean. Aquarium director Rob Yarrell called Inky a "curious boy," explaining that octopuses are by nature very intelligent "escape artists."

# #JUSTICEFORHARAMBE
## Meme honors slain gorilla

The killing of Cincinnati Zoo's gorilla Harambe in May 2016 was a tragic event that spawned one of the year's most pervasive memes. Twitter users soon began posting images of Harambe photoshopped alongside the many celebrities who passed away in 2016, or tweeting song lyrics with Harambe's name incorporated. The meme reached a peak in August 2016 when a user hacked zoo director Thane Maynard's Twitter account to tweet about Harambe. Activity still hadn't died down by November, when many Twitter users claimed to have voted for the gorilla in the U.S. presidential election.

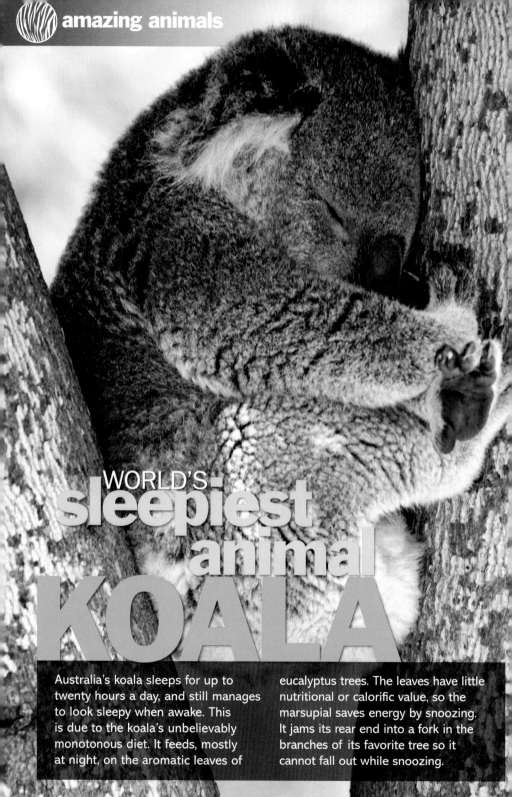

# WORLD'S sleepiest animal KOALA

Australia's koala sleeps for up to twenty hours a day, and still manages to look sleepy when awake. This is due to the koala's unbelievably monotonous diet. It feeds, mostly at night, on the aromatic leaves of eucalyptus trees. The leaves have little nutritional or calorific value, so the marsupial saves energy by snoozing. It jams its rear end into a fork in the branches of its favorite tree so it cannot fall out while snoozing.

# WORLD'S
# best glider

Flying squirrels are champion animal gliders. The Japanese giant flying squirrel has been scientifically recorded making flights of up to 164 feet from tree to tree. These creatures have been estimated to make 656-foot flights when flying downhill. The squirrel remains aloft using a special flap of skin on either side of its body, which stretches between wrist and ankle. Its fluffy tail acts as a stabilizer to keep it steady, and the squirrel changes direction by twisting its wrists and moving its limbs.

# FLYING SQUIRREL

## WORLD'S GLIDERS
Distance in feet

Flying squirrel 656

Flying fish 655

Colugo, or flying lemur 230

Draco flying lizard 197

Flying squid 164

# WORLD'S heaviest land mammal

# AFRICAN ELEPHANT

The African bush elephant is the world's largest living land animal. The biggest known bush stood 13.8 feet at the shoulder and had an estimated weight of 13.5 tons. It is also the animal with the largest outer ears. The outsized flappers help to keep the animal cool on the open savanna. The Asian elephant has much smaller earflaps, because it lives in the forest and is not exposed to the same high temperatures.

# WORLD'S
# tiniest bat
# KITTI'S
# HOG-NOSED
# BAT

This little critter, the Kitti's hog-nosed bat, is just 1.3 inches long, with a wingspan of 6.7 inches, and weighs 0.07–0.10 ounces. It's tied for first place as world's smallest animal with Savi's pygmy shrew, which is longer at 2.1 inches but lighter at 0.04–0.06 ounces. The bat lives in west central Thailand and southeast Myanmar, and the shrew is found from the Mediterranean to Southeast Asia.

131

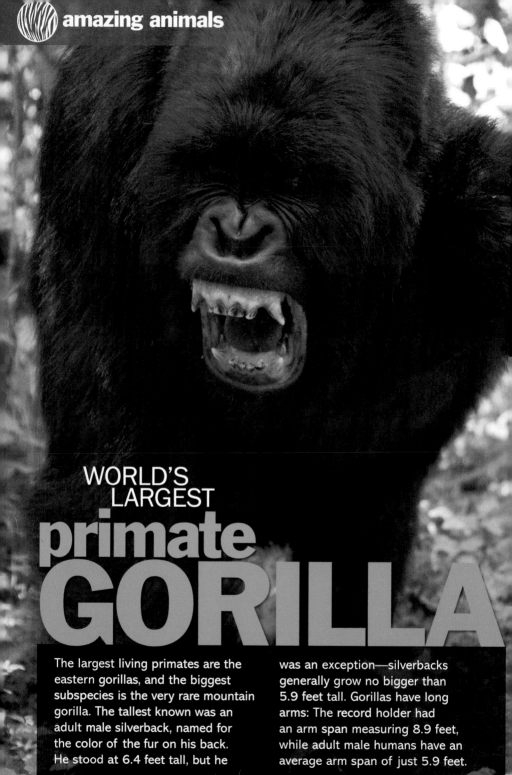

## WORLD'S LARGEST
# primate
# GORILLA

The largest living primates are the eastern gorillas, and the biggest subspecies is the very rare mountain gorilla. The tallest known was an adult male silverback, named for the color of the fur on his back. He stood at 6.4 feet tall, but he was an exception—silverbacks generally grow no bigger than 5.9 feet tall. Gorillas have long arms: The record holder had an arm span measuring 8.9 feet, while adult male humans have an average arm span of just 5.9 feet.

# MOST COLORFUL monkey in the world
# MANDRILL

The male mandrill's face is as flamboyant as his rear end. The vivid colors of both are brightest at breeding time. The colors announce to his rivals that he is an alpha male and he has the right to breed with the females. His exceptionally long and fang-like canine teeth reinforce his dominance. As his colors fade, so does his success with the ladies. Even so, he is still the world's largest monkey, as well as the most colorful.

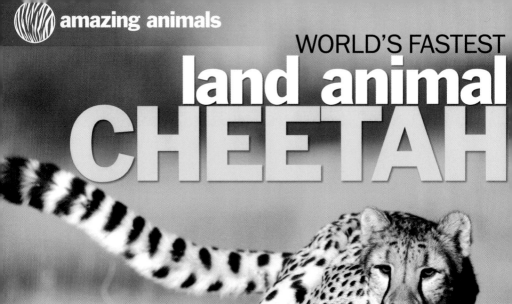

# WORLD'S FASTEST
# land animal
# CHEETAH

The fastest reliably recorded running speed of any animal was that of a zoo-bred cheetah that reached an incredible 65 miles per hour on a flat surface. Another captive cheetah, this time at Cincinnati Zoo, clocked 61 miles per hour from a standing start in 2012.

More recently, wild cheetahs have been timed while actually hunting their prey in the bush in Botswana. Using GPS technology and special tracking collars, the scientists found that these cheetahs had a top speed of 58 miles per hour over rough terrain.

## FASTEST LAND ANIMALS
Speed in miles per hour

**Cheetah 65**

**African ostrich 60**

**Pronghorn 55**

**Springbok 55**

**Lion 30**

# WORLD'S FASTEST fish
# BLACK MARLIN

Timing the world's fastest fish relies on how fast a hooked fish pulls the line from a fisherman's reel, so part of its escape is by swimming and part by leaping. Using this method, sailfish, marlin, and swordfish come out on top. The sailfish was credited with 68 miles per hour in the 1930s.

A BBC film crew claimed 80 miles per hour for a black marlin in 2001. Then, in a computer simulation in Japan in 2008, scientists calculated that a swordfish could reach 81 miles per hour. But this has not yet been proven in real trials, so the black marlin stays on top for now.

# WORLD'S BIGGEST big cat

# TIGER

Big cats are the only cats that roar. There are five of them: tiger, lion, jaguar, leopard, and snow leopard. The biggest and heaviest is the Siberian, or Amur, tiger, which lives in the taiga (forestland) of eastern Siberia, where it hunts deer and wild boar. The largest reliably measured tigers have been about 11.8 feet long and weighed 705 pounds, but there have been claims for larger individuals, such as the male shot in the Sikhote-Alin Mountains in 1950. That tiger weighed 847 pounds.

# WORLD'S NOISIEST
# land animal
# HOWLER MONKEY

The howler monkeys of Latin America are deafening. Males have an especially large hyoid. This horseshoe-shaped bone in the neck creates a chamber that makes the monkey's deep guttural growls sound louder for longer. It is said that their calls can be heard up to 3 miles away. Both males and females call, and they holler mainly in the morning. It is thought that these calls are often one troop telling neighboring troops where they are.

**REACHING GREAT HEIGHTS**
A giraffe's tongue can grow up to 21 inches in length. This helps the animal to reach leaves on the topmost branches of a tree when it is looking for food.

WORLD'S
TALLEST
living animal
GIRAFFE

## GIRAFFE STATS

# 6
**HEIGHT OF A CALF AT BIRTH: 6 feet**

# 25
**AVERAGE LIFE SPAN: 25 years**

# 100
**ADULT'S DAILY FOOD CONSUMPTION:
100 pounds of leaves and twigs**

Giraffes living on the savannas of East and southern Africa are the world's tallest animals. The tallest known bull giraffe measured 19 feet from the ground to the top of his horns. He could have looked over the top of a London double-decker bus or peered into the upstairs window of a two-story house. Despite having considerably longer necks than we do, giraffes have the same number of neck vertebrae. They also have long legs with which they can either speedily escape from predators, or kick them to keep them away.

# WORLD'S LONGEST tooth
# NARWHAL

The narwhal's "sword" is an enormously elongated spiral tooth, or tusk. It can grow to more than 8.2 feet long. Several functions have been suggested for the tusk, from an adornment to attract the opposite sex—like a peacock's tail—to a sensory organ that detects changes in the seawater, such as saltiness, which could help the narwhal find food. Observers have noted that the larger a male narwhal's tusk, the more attractive he is to females.

# THE WORLD'S LARGEST
# animal...ever
# BLUE WHALE

Blue whales are truly colossal. The largest one accurately measured was 110 feet long, and the heaviest weighed 209 tons. They feed on tiny krill, which they filter from the sea. On land, the largest known animal was a Titanosaur—a huge dinosaur that lived in what is now Argentina 101 million years ago. A skeleton found in 2014 suggests the creature was 121 feet long and weighed 77 tons. It belongs to a young Titanosaur, so an adult may have been bigger than a

# WORLD'S BIGGEST fish
# WHALE SHARK

Recognizable from its spotted skin and enormous size, the whale shark is the world's largest living fish. It grows to a maximum length of about 66 feet. Like the blue whale, this mega fish feeds on some of the smallest fish: krill, marine larvae, small fish, and fish eggs. The whale shark is also a great traveler: One female was tracked swimming 4,800 miles from Mexico—where hundreds of whale sharks gather each summer to feed—to the middle of the South Atlantic Ocean, where it is thought she may have given birth.

# THE SHARK MOST DANGEROUS
## to people
# GREAT WHITE SHARK

## SHARK ATTACKS
Number of humans attacked

**Great white 314**

**Tiger shark 111**

**Bull shark 100**

**Sand tiger 29**

The great white shark is at the top of the list for the highest number of attacks on people. The largest reliably measured fish was 21 feet long, making it the largest predatory fish in the sea. Its jaws are lined with large, triangular, serrated teeth that can slice through flesh, sinew, and even bone. However, there were just 314 reported nonprovoked attacks between 1580 and 2014, so humans cannot be this creature's top food of choice. People don't have enough fat on their bodies. Mature white sharks prefer blubber-rich seals, dolphins, and whales. It is likely that many of the attacks on people are probably cases of mistaken identity.

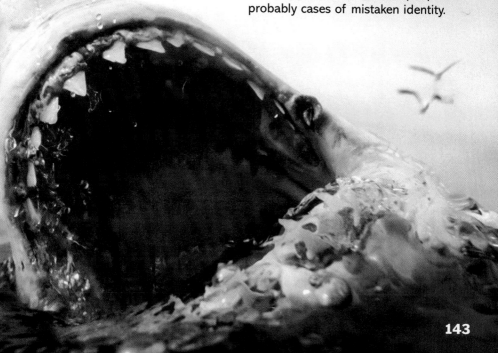

WORLD'S
LARGEST
# crustacean
# JAPANESE
# SPIDER
# CRAB

The deepwater Japanese spider crab has the largest leg span of any known crab or lobster. It comes a close second to the American lobster (the world's heaviest crustacean) by weight, and its gangly limbs can be extraordinarily long. The first European to discover this species found two sets of claws, measuring 10 feet long, propped up against a fisherman's hut. The crab must have been about 22 feet from one claw tip to the other when its limbs were spread apart.

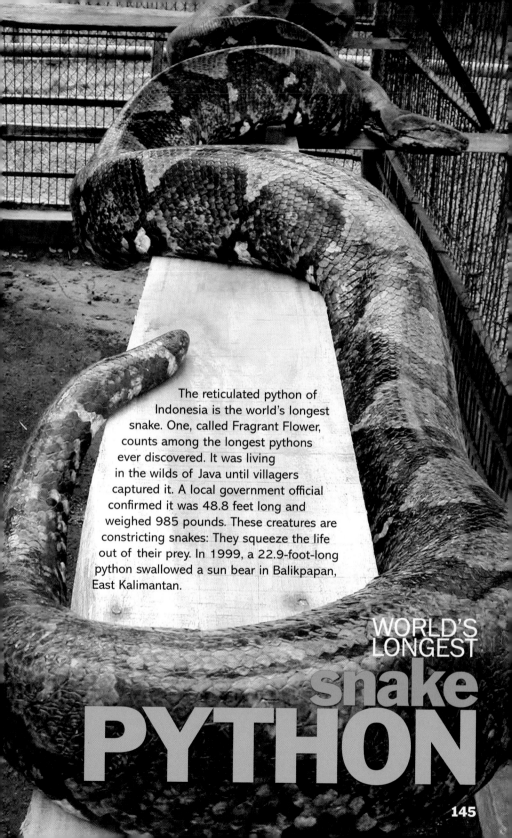

The reticulated python of Indonesia is the world's longest snake. One, called Fragrant Flower, counts among the longest pythons ever discovered. It was living in the wilds of Java until villagers captured it. A local government official confirmed it was 48.8 feet long and weighed 985 pounds. These creatures are constricting snakes: They squeeze the life out of their prey. In 1999, a 22.9-foot-long python swallowed a sun bear in Balikpapan, East Kalimantan.

## WORLD'S LONGEST snake PYTHON

amazing animals

## WORLD'S
# largest lizard

# KOMODO DRAGON

There are dragons on Indonesia's Komodo Island, and they're dangerous. The Komodo dragon's jaws are lined with sixty replaceable, serrated, backward-pointing teeth. Its saliva is laced with deadly bacteria and venom that the dragon works into a wound, ensuring its prey will die quickly. Prey can be as big as a pig or deer, because this lizard is the world's largest. It can grow up to 10.3 feet long and weigh 366 pounds.

# WORLD'S
# deadliest frog

## POISON DART FROG

A poison dart frog's skin exudes toxins. There are several species, and the more vivid a frog's color, the more deadly its poison. The skin color warns potential predators that the frogs are not good to eat, although one snake is immune to the chemicals and happily feeds on these creatures. It is thought that the frogs do not manufacture their own poisons, but obtain the chemicals from their diet of ants, millipedes, and mites. The most deadly species to people is also the largest, Colombia's golden poison dart frog. At just one inch long, a single frog has enough poison to kill ten to twenty people.

**amazing animals**

# WORLD'S LARGEST
# reptile
# SALTWATER
# CROCODILE

The saltwater crocodile, or "saltie," is the world's largest living reptile. Males can grow to over 20 feet long, but a few old-timers become real monsters. A well-known crocodile in the Segama River, Borneo, left an impression on a sandbank that measured 33 feet. The saltie can be found in areas from eastern India to northeast Australia, where it lives in mangroves, estuaries, and rivers. It is sometimes found out at sea. The saltie is an ambush predator, grabbing any animal that enters its domain—including people. Saltwater crocodiles account for twenty to thirty attacks on people per year, up to half of which are fatal.

**"SALTIE"** crocodiles can live for up to 70 years in the wild.

**148**

# WORLD'S SMALLEST owl
# NORTH AMERICAN ELF OWL

## WORLD'S SMALLEST OWLS
Height in inches

| North American elf owl 5 | Little owl 8.7 | Barn owl 15 | Snowy owl 28 | Great gray owl 33 |

The North American elf owl is one of three tiny owls vying for this title. It is about 5 inches long and weighs 1.5 ounces. This owl spends winter in Mexico and flies to nest in Arizona and New Mexico in spring. It often occupies cavities excavated by woodpeckers in saguaro cacti. Rivals for the title of smallest owl are Peru's long-whiskered owlet and Mexico's Tamaulipas pygmy owl, which are both a touch shorter but slightly heavier, making the elf owl the smallest of all.

# WORLD'S
# smelliest
## bird
# HOATZIN

The hoatzin eats leaves, flowers, and fruit, and ferments the food in its crop. This habit leaves the bird with a foul odor, which has led people to nickname the hoatzin the "stinkbird." About the size of a pheasant, this bird lives in the Amazon and Orinoco river basins of South America. The hoatzin chick has sharp claws on its wings, like a pterodactyl. If threatened by a snake, the chick jumps from the nest into the water, then uses its wing claws to help it climb back up.

# bird with the
## LONGEST TAIL
# RIBBON-TAILED ASTRAPIA

The ribbon-tailed astrapia has the longest feathers in relation to body size of any wild bird. The male, which has a beautiful, iridescent blue-green head, sports a pair of white ribbon-shaped tail feathers that are more than 3.3 feet long—three times the length of its 13-inch-long body. It is one of Papua New Guinea's birds of paradise and lives in the mountain forests of central New Guinea, where males sometimes have to untangle their tails from the foliage before they can fly.

# BIRD WITH THE LONGEST wingspan
# WANDERING ALBATROSS

Long, narrow wings, like those of a glider aircraft, are the mark of the wandering albatross. The longest authenticated measurement for wingspan was taken in 1965 from an old-timer, its pure-white plumage an indication of its age. Its wingspan was 11.9 feet. This seabird rarely flaps its wings, but uses the wind and updrafts from waves to soar effortlessly over the ocean.

## BIRDS WITH LONG WINGSPANS
Wingspan in feet

Wandering albatross 11.9

Great white pelican 11.81

Andean condor 10.5

Marabou stork 10.5

Southern royal albatross 9.8

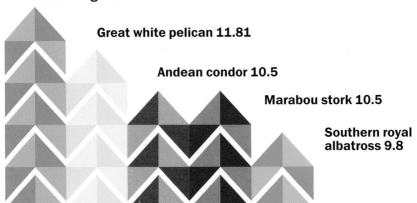

# BIRD WITH THE STRONGEST
## forehead

The helmeted hornbill is a real bruiser. It has a structure, known as a casque, sitting atop its chisel-like bill. Unlike other hornbills, which have hollow casques, the helmeted hornbill has an almost solid one. It is filled with "hornbill ivory," which is even more valuable than elephant ivory in southern Asia. The bill and casque weigh more than 10 percent of the bird's body weight. Males use their heads as battering rams, slamming casques together in fights over territory.

# HELMETED HORNBILL

# BIRD THAT BUILDS largest nest BALD EAGLE

## THE WORLD'S LARGEST NESTS
Diameter in inches

Bald eagle 114

Golden eagle 55

White stork 57

With a wingspan over 6.6 feet, bald eagles need space to land and take off—so their nests can be gargantuan. Over the years, a nest built by a pair of bald eagles in St. Petersburg, Florida, has taken on epic proportions. Measuring 9.5 feet across and 20 feet deep, it is made of sticks, grass, and moss. At one stage it was thought to have weighed at least 2 tons, making it the largest nest ever constructed by a pair of birds. Although only one pair nests at any one time, these huge structures are often the work of several pairs of birds, each building on top of the work of their predecessors.

5.9 in

4.5 in

WORLD'S
# largest bird egg
# AFRICAN
# OSTRICH
# EGG

The African ostrich lays the largest eggs of any living bird, yet they are the smallest eggs relative to the size of the mother's body. Each egg is some 5.9 inches long and weighs about 3.5–5 pounds, while the mother is about 6.2 feet tall and the male 1.6 feet taller, making the ostrich the world's largest living bird. The female lays about fifty eggs per year, and each egg contains as much yolk and albumen as twenty-four hens' eggs. It takes an hour to soft boil an ostrich egg!

# EMPEROR PENGUIN STATS

## 80

AVERAGE WEIGHT OF AN ADULT:
80 pounds

## 1,640

DEPTHS AN ADULT CAN SWIM TO:
1,640 feet

## 22

LENGTH OF TIME UNDERWATER:
Up to 22 minutes

**WORLD'S TALLEST PENGUINS**
Height in inches

Emperor 48    King 39    Gentoo 35    Macaroni 28    Galápagos 19

# WORLD'S BIGGEST
# penguin

# EMPEROR PENGUIN

At 4 feet tall, the emperor penguin is the world's biggest living penguin. It has a most curious lifestyle, breeding during the long, dark Antarctic winter. The female lays a single egg and carefully passes it to the male. She heads out to sea to feed, while he remains with the egg balanced on his feet and tucked under a fold of blubber-rich skin. There he stands with all the other penguin dads, huddled together to keep warm in the blizzards and 20-mile-per-hour winds that scour the icy continent. Come spring, the egg hatches, the female returns, and mom and dad swap duties, taking turns to feed and care for their fluffy chick.

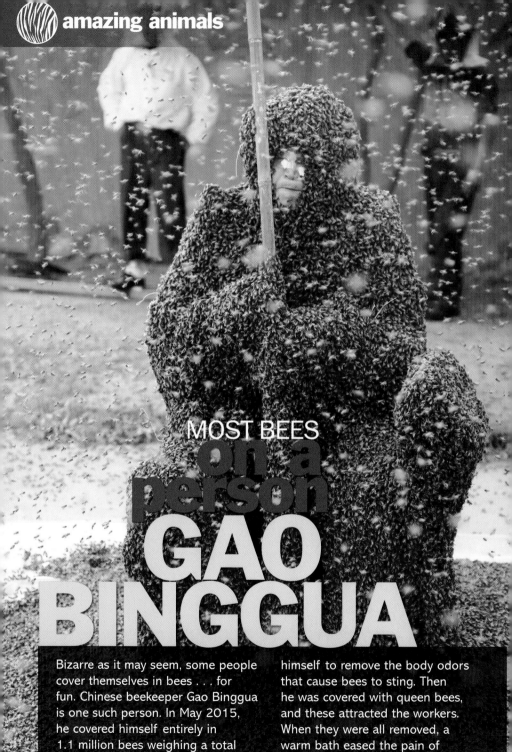

# MOST BEES on a person
## GAO BINGGUA

Bizarre as it may seem, some people cover themselves in bees . . . for fun. Chinese beekeeper Gao Binggua is one such person. In May 2015, he covered himself entirely in 1.1 million bees weighing a total of 240 pounds. First he washed himself to remove the body odors that cause bees to sting. Then he was covered with queen bees, and these attracted the workers. When they were all removed, a warm bath eased the pain of two thousand–plus bee stings!

# WORLD'S FASTEST
# flying insect
# DESERT LOCUST

Flying insects are difficult to clock, and many crazy speeds have been claimed. The fastest airspeed reliably timed was by fifteen desert locusts that managed an average of 21 miles per hour. Airspeed is the actual speed at which the insect flies. It is different from ground speed, which is often enhanced by favorable winds.

A black cutworm moth whizzed along at 70 miles per hour while riding the winds ahead of a cold front. The most shocking measurement, however, is that of a horsefly with an estimated airspeed of 90 miles per hour while chasing an air-gun pellet! The speed, understandably, has not been verified.

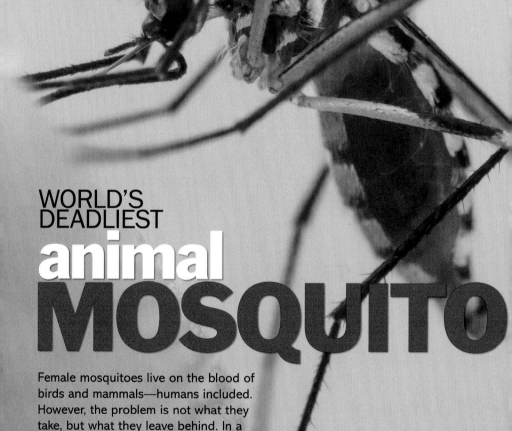

# WORLD'S DEADLIEST
# animal
# MOSQUITO

Female mosquitoes live on the blood of birds and mammals—humans included. However, the problem is not what they take, but what they leave behind. In a mosquito's saliva are organisms that cause the world's most deadly illnesses, including malaria, yellow fever, dengue fever, West Nile virus, and encephalitis. It is estimated that mosquitoes transmit diseases to a staggering 700 million people every year, of which 725,000 die. Mosquitoes are the most deadly family of insects on Earth.

# WORLD'S HEAVIEST spider
# GOLIATH BIRD-EATING TARANTULA

## SPIDERS WITH THE LARGEST LEG SPANS
Span in inches

**Giant huntsman spider 12**

**Goliath bird-eating tarantula 11**

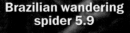

**Brazilian wandering spider 5.9**

**Golden silk orb-weaver 5**

The size of a dinner plate, the female goliath bird-eating tarantula has a leg span of 11 inches and weighs up to 6.17 ounces. This is the world's heaviest spider and a real nightmare for an arachnophobe (someone with a fear of spiders). Its fangs can pierce a person's skin, but its venom is no worse than a bee sting. The hairs on its body are more of a hazard. When threatened, it rubs its abdomen with its hind legs and releases tiny hairs that cause severe irritation to the skin. Despite its name, this spider does not actually eat birds very often.

# amazing animals

## PET ANIMALS
# TRENDING #

### FAMOUS FEATHERS
Chicken struts his stuff in blue shorts

A bizarre video of a chicken went viral in 2016, after the bird's owner, Debra Snodgrass, filmed "Charlie" running around her Arizona farmyard wearing bright blue shorts. The shorts were not the only interesting fashion choice for the humble chicken: Snodgrass originally posted the video to Facebook with the caption, "Connor and I also painted his nails last night. He was feelin' good with his nails did and new pants."

### CANINE CONSPIRACY
Hank sparks controversy

The Milwaukee Brewers were forced to hold a press conference in 2016 to confirm that their unofficial mascot "Hank the ballpark pup" was really Hank. New pictures had shown Hank looking remarkably different, leading conspiracy theorists to believe that the original dog had been replaced by an imposter—even after the Brewers produced the dog's veterinary records. Hank has been a beloved part of the Brewers' family since arriving as a stray at Maryvale Baseball Park during 2014 spring training.

## 10/10
### Top ratings account

2016 saw a rise in "ratings" Twitter accounts, inspired by the popular account called WeRateDogs, which invites users to submit pictures of their furry friends, along with ratings out of ten and funny explanations. A lizard-rating account became the second most popular pet-rating account after joining Twitter in January 2016, and it now has over 28,000 followers. WeRateDogs, in comparison, has more than a million followers, and now has a website, store, and mobile app.

# COOL FOR CATS
## Jesperpus braves the snow

Three-year-old cat Jesperpus became famous in April 2016 after owner Aina Stormo filmed him accompanying her cross-country skiing near Hedmark, Norway, for

*National Geographic.* Jesper, who apparently loves winter sports, not only stars on his own YouTube channel, but also has more than 16,000 followers on Instagram and 40,000 on Facebook. He released a book and a calendar in 2017.

# BEST DRESSED
## Polly's new look

New Jersey goat shelter Goats of Anarchy posted an adorable picture to their Instagram feed in 2016, featuring six-month-old Polly, a blind goat with anxiety and other neurological problems. The shelter found an innovative way to help Polly feel safe and fall asleep— by dressing her in a child's duck costume! Polly and her outfit are now a regular feature on the shelter's Instagram account.

# WORLD'S FLUFFIEST
# rabbit
# ANGORA RABBIT

In most people's opinion, the Angora rabbit is the world's fluffiest bunny. The breed originated in Turkey and is thought to be one of the world's oldest rabbits as well. It became popular with the French court in the mid-eighteenth century. Today it is bred for its long, soft, white wool, which is shorn every three to four months throughout the year. One of the fluffiest bunnies must be Ida. In 2014, she won "Best in Show" at the American Rabbit Breeders Association National Convention, the first Angora ever to do so.

Thumbelina is a dwarf miniature horse. At just 17.5 inches tall and weighing 60 pounds, she is officially the world's smallest horse. She is stout with unusually short limbs, a far cry from the long-limbed Big Jake, the world's tallest horse: a Belgian gelding at 6.9 feet.

# THE WORLD'S SMALLEST horse
# THUMBELINA

# WORLD'S HAIRIEST dog
# KOMONDOR

The world's hairiest dog breed is the komondor, or Hungarian sheepdog. It is a powerful dog that was bred originally to guard sheep. Its long, white, dreadlock-like "cords" enable it not only to blend in with the flock, but also to protect itself from bad weather and bites from wolves. This is a large dog, standing over 27.5 inches at the shoulders. Its hairs are up to 10.6 inches long, giving it the heaviest coat of any dog.

# AMERICA'S MOST POPULAR dog breed
# LABRADOR

The Labrador retriever holds the top spot as America's most popular breed of dog for a record-breaking 26th consecutive year. Its eager-to-please temperament makes it an ideal companion. The Labrador was originally bred as a gun dog that fetched game birds shot by hunters. Now, aside from being a family pet, it is a favored assistance dog that helps blind people, and a good detection dog used by law-enforcement agencies.

## AMERICA'S MOST POPULAR DOGS
Rating
1 LABRADOR
2 GERMAN SHEPHERD
3 GOLDEN RETRIEVER
4 BULLDOG
5 BEAGLE
6 FRENCH BULLDOG
7 POODLE
8 ROTTWEILER
9 YORKSHIRE TERRIER
10 BOXER

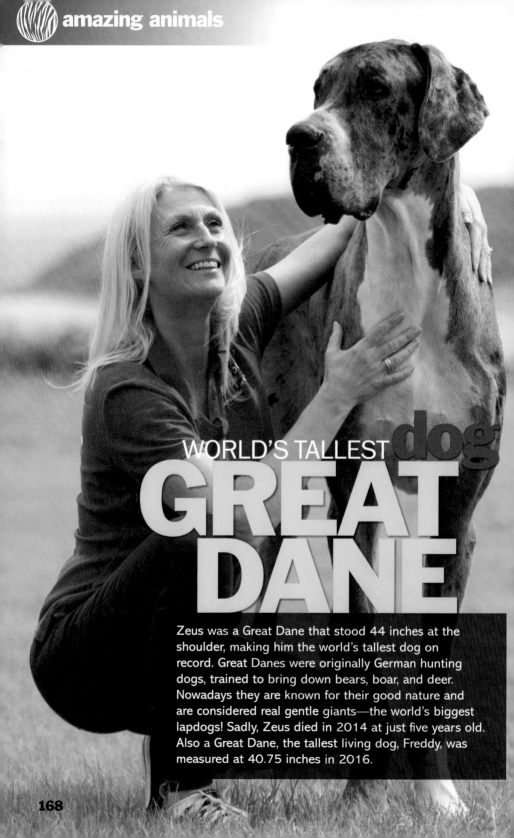

# WORLD'S TALLEST dog
# GREAT DANE

Zeus was a Great Dane that stood 44 inches at the shoulder, making him the world's tallest dog on record. Great Danes were originally German hunting dogs, trained to bring down bears, boar, and deer. Nowadays they are known for their good nature and are considered real gentle giants—the world's biggest lapdogs! Sadly, Zeus died in 2014 at just five years old. Also a Great Dane, the tallest living dog, Freddy, was measured at 40.75 inches in 2016.

# WORLD'S

Chihuahuas are the world's smallest dog breed—and the smallest of them all is Miracle Milly, a Chihuahua from Puerto Rico. She measures just 3.8 inches tall, no bigger than a sneaker. The shortest is Heaven Sent Brandy from Florida, just 6 inches from her nose to the tip of her tail. Chihuahuas originated in Mexico, and may have predated the Maya. They are probably descendants of the Techichi, an early companion dog of the Toltec civilization (900–1168 C.E.).

## smallest dog

# CHIHUAHUA

# amazing animals

## AMERICA'S MOST POPULAR
## cat breed
## EXOTIC SHORTHAIR

The exotic has done it again! It is America's most popular breed of 2016, the third year in a row, according to the Cat Fanciers' Association. Its thick, short coat, giving the cat a teddy bear look, is easier to manage than the long coat of the Persian, and its round, Garfield-like face is as appealing as the cartoon cat itself. A calm and friendly breed, the exotic shorthair is also recognized as an accomplished "mouser." The Ragdoll and British Shorthair, meanwhile, have pushed the Persian, once the top cat, into fourth place.

**America's most popular cats**
Rating

1 EXOTIC SHORTHAIR
2 RAGDOLL
3 BRITISH SHORTHAIR
4 PERSIAN
5 MAINE COON CAT
6 AMERICAN SHORTHAIR
7 SCOTTISH FOLD
8 SPHYNX
9 ABYSSINIAN
10 DEVON REX

# WORLD'S BALDEST cat

# SPHYNX

The sphynx breed of cats is famous for its wrinkles and the lack of a normal coat, but it is not entirely hairless. Its skin is like the softest chamois leather, but it has a thin layer of down. It behaves more like when they come home, and is friendly to strangers. The breed originated in Canada, where a black-and-white cat gave birth to a hairless kitten called Prune in 1966. Subsequent breeding gave rise to

**7**

incredible
EARTH

# INCREDIBLE EARTH
# TRENDING #

## EARTH LOVE
Most followed noncelebrity Instagram

*National Geographic*'s Instagram was once again the most followed noncelebrity Instagram account in 2016, with more than sixty-two million followers and one billion likes across its more than 12,000 posts. The account is so successful that, in November 2016, the National Geographic Museum opened an exhibition entitled "@NatGeo: The Most Popular Instagram Photos" to showcase the best and most liked images from the ever-popular Instagram feed.

## PEAK PHOTOGRAPHY
Most dangerous photo op

Rio de Janeiro's Pedra da Gávea mountain has become a top destination for tourists searching for the perfect adventure photograph. At 2,762 feet above sea level, the mountain is one of the world's highest, and while the cliff is undoubtedly picturesque, it is also an incredibly dangerous spot for selfies and other photography. Intrepid travelers have become increasingly more daring with their shots on the mountain, some even photographing themselves with selfie sticks as they hang from the ledge.

## ON THE SLOPES
### Most popular North American ski resort

According to Facebook, Whistler Blackcomb is the most popular ski resort in North America, with over 1.2 million people expressing interest in it via the social networking site. The "four season mountain resort" near Vancouver, in British Columbia, Canada, was also named the top ski resort in North America by *SKI Magazine* in 2016, for the third year in a row.

## HAPPY BIRTHDAY!
### 100 years of the National Park Service

The National Park Service turned one hundred in August 2016, and its centennial year proved one of its most popular yet, with a record-breaking 331 million visits to its parks. The most popular national park in 2016 was California's Golden Gate National Recreation Area, home of the impressive redwood trees, which had more than 15.6 million visitors.

## @HAWAIIREEF
### Obama's big conservation project

Papahānaumokuākea, an archipelago off the coast of Hawaii, became the largest protected natural area on Earth in 2016, when outgoing U.S. President Barack Obama extended the protected area by a whopping 200 miles in each direction. The archipelago is home to some of the Earth's oldest, rarest, and most endangered species—including Hawaiian monk seals and a 4,000-year-old black coral reef.

# incredible earth

## trees on earth OLDEST
# BRISTLECONE PINE

An unnamed bristlecone pine in the White Mountains of California is the world's oldest continually standing tree. It is 5,062 years old, beating its bristlecone rivals the Methuselah at 4,845 years old and Prometheus at 4,844 years old. Sweden is home to an even older tree, a Norway spruce (which are often used as Christmas trees) that took root about 9,550 years ago. However, this tree has not been standing continually, but is long-lived because it can clone itself. When the trunk dies, a new one grows up from the same rootstock, so in theory it could live forever.

# WORLD'S TALLEST tree
# CALIFORNIA REDWOOD

A coast redwood named Hyperion is the world's tallest known living tree. It is 379.1 feet tall, and could have grown taller if a woodpecker had not hammered its top. It's growing in a remote part of the Redwood National and State Parks in Northern California, but its exact location is kept a secret for fear that too many visitors would upset its ecosystem. It is thought to be 700 to 800 years old.

## WORLD'S TALLEST TREES
Height in feet

California redwood, California, USA 379.1

Mountain ash, Tasmania 327.4

Coast Douglas fir, Oregon, USA 327.3

Sitka spruce, California, USA 317

Giant sequoia, California, USA 314

# LARGEST AND HEAVIEST fruit

The world's largest-ever fruit was a cultivated pumpkin grown by Swiss gardener Beni Meier, the first non-American giant pumpkin champion. His winning squash weighed an incredible 2,324 pounds, and Beni had to hire special transportation to take it for weighing in at the European Championship Pumpkin Weigh-off, held in Germany in October 2014. The seeds of nearly all giant pumpkins can trace their ancestry back to a species of squash that was cultivated by Canadian pumpkin breeder Howard Dill.

# PUMPKIN

# WORLD'S TOUGHEST leaf
# AMAZON WATER LILY

The leaf of the giant Amazon water lily is up to 8.6 feet across. It has an upturned rim and a waxy, water-repellent upper surface. On the underside of the leaf is a strong, riblike structure that traps air between the ribs so that the leaf floats easily. The ribs are also lined with sharp spines to protect them from aquatic plant eaters. The leaf is so large and so strong that it can support the weight of a child.

# WORLD'S LARGEST
# single flower
# RAFFLESIA

The scent of dead and decaying meat is not the usual quality sought in a flower, but the flies and beetles on the islands of Borneo and Sumatra love it. *Rafflesia* is known locally as the corpse flower, and at 3.3 feet across, it is the world's largest. It has no obvious stems, leaves, or roots because it is a parasite, and the only time anyone sees it is when it flowers. A female flower has to be fairly close to a male flower for successful pollination, and that is rare, because groups of flowers tend to be either one gender or the other. With forests on the two islands dwindling, the future for *Rafflesia* looks bleak.

WORLD'S MOST
DANGEROUS
# mushroom
# DEATH
# CAP

Don't eat the death cap—the warning is in the name. This fungus is responsible for the most deaths by mushroom poisoning and can be found all over the world, including the United States. The mushroom's toxins damage the liver and kidneys, and it is not possible to destroy the dangerous chemicals by cooking, freezing, or drying. The Roman emperor Claudius is thought to have died from death-cap poisoning in 54 C.E. He liked to eat a salad of Caesar mushrooms, an almost identical edible species, but was served up the killer fungus instead.

## EXTRAORDINARY LENGTHS
In order to establish the record-breaking depths of Krubera Cave, diver Gennady Samokhin had to descend to a depth of 151 feet in an underwater channel.

The limestone-rich Western Caucasus in Abkhazia have some extraordinary cave systems. Among the caverns there is Krubera, the deepest-known cave on Earth. Explorers have descended 7,208 feet from the cave entrance, and they suspect there is even more to explore. The cave is named for the Russian geographer Alexander Kruber, but the Ukrainian cave explorers have dubbed it "Crows' Cave" on account of the number of crows that nest around the entrance.

DEEPEST CAVE
on earth
KRUBERA

## KRUBERA CAVE STATS

# 1963
YEAR OF DISCOVERY: 1963

# 7,208
DEPTH DISCOVERED TO DATE:
7,208 feet

# 2012
YEAR CURRENT DEPTH DISCOVERED
ESTABLISHED: 2012

# THE LARGEST CUT
# diamond
# GOLDEN JUBILEE

In 1985, South African miners chanced upon an enormous diamond. Jewel specialists worked for many years to hone it to perfection and fashioned a gem that was a staggering 545.67 carats, the largest cut diamond in the world. Pope John Paul II blessed the jewel, and the Thai royal family now owns it. For some time, the gem was known as Unnamed Brown, on account of its color. Today it goes by the name of Golden Jubilee. If the diamond had been colorless, it would have been worth over $14 million—however, it is a yellow-brown color and worth "only" about $12 million.

# GREATEST NUMBER
# of geysers
# YELLOWSTONE
# NATIONAL
# PARK

There are about 1,000 geysers that erupt worldwide, and 540 of them are in Yellowstone National Park, USA. That's the greatest concentration of geysers on Earth. The most famous is Old Faithful, which spews out a cloud of steam and hot water to a maximum height of 185 feet every 44 to 125 minutes. Yellowstone's spectacular water display is due to its closeness to molten rock from Earth's mantle that rises up to the surface. One day the park could face an eruption one thousand times as powerful as that of Mt. St. Helens in 1980.

## GEYSER FIELDS
Number of geysers

Yellowstone, Idaho, Montana, Wyoming, USA 540

Valley of Geysers, Kamchatka, Russia 139

El Tatio, Andes, Chile 84

Orakei Korako, New Zealand 33

Hveravellir, Iceland 16

# 29,029 feet

Mount Everest's snowy peak is an unbelievable 5.5 miles above sea level. This mega mountain is located in the Himalayas, on the border between Tibet and Nepal. The mountain acquired its official name from surveyor Sir George Everest, but local people know it as Chomolungma (Tibet) and Sagarmatha (Nepal). In 1953, Sir Edmund Hillary and Sherpa Tenzing Norgay were the first to reach its summit. Now, more than 650 people per year manage to make the spectacular climb.

# MOUNT EVEREST is earth's TALLEST MOUNTAIN above sea level

## HIMALAYAN MOUNTAINS
Height above sea level in feet

Everest 29,029

K2 (Qogir) 28,251

Kanchenjunga 28,179

Lhotse 27,940

Makalu 27,838

# WORLD'S GREATEST
## barrier
# REEF

Australia's Great Barrier Reef is the only living thing that's clearly visible from space. It stretches along the Queensland coast for 1,400 miles, making it the largest coral reef system in the world. The reef is home to an astounding number of animals: over 600 species of corals alone, 133 species of sharks and rays, and 30 species of whales and dolphins. In recent years, climate change has posed a huge threat to the world's coral reefs, with rising sea temperatures causing areas to die off. The northern half of the Great Barrier Reef suffered particularly in 2016 and scientists fear that more damage is yet to come.

## WORLD'S LONGEST BARRIER REEFS
Length in miles

**Great Barrier Reef, Australia 1,400**

**New Caledonia Barrier Reef, South Pacific 930**

**Mesoamerican Barrier Reef, Caribbean 620**

**Ningaloo Reef, Western Australia 162**

# incredible earth

## WORLD'S LARGEST
# hot desert
# SAHARA
# DESERT

Sahara means simply "great desert," and great it is: It is the largest hot desert on the planet. It's the size of the United States and China combined, and dominates North Africa from the Atlantic Ocean in the west to the Red Sea in the east. It's extremely dry, with most of the Sahara receiving less than 0.1 inches of rain a year, and some places none at all for several years. It is stiflingly hot, up to 122°F, making it one of the hottest and driest regions in the world.

## WORLD'S LARGEST HOT DESERTS
Size in square miles

**Sahara Desert, North Africa
3.63 million**

**Arabian Desert, Western Asia
900,000**

**Great Victoria Desert, Australia 250,000**

**Kalahari Desert, Africa
220,000**

**Syrian Desert, Arabian peninsula
190,000**

# WORLD'S LARGEST lake
# CASPIAN SEA

Russia, Kazakhstan, Turkmenistan, Iran, and Azerbaijan border the vast Caspian Sea, the largest inland body of water on Earth. Once part of an ancient sea, the lake became landlocked between five and ten million years ago, with occasional fills of salt water as sea levels fluctuated over time. Now it has a surface area of about 149,200 square miles and is home to one of the world's most valuable fish: the beluga sturgeon, the source of beluga caviar, which costs up to $2,250 per pound.

## WORLD'S LARGEST LAKES
Area in square miles

Caspian Sea, Europe/ Asia 149,200

Lake Superior, North America 31,700

Lake Victoria, Africa 26,600

Lake Huron, North America 23,000

Lake Michigan, North America 22,300

incredible earth

# WORLD'S LONGEST river
# NILE RIVER

People who study rivers cannot agree on the Nile's source— nobody knows where it actually starts. Some say the most likely source is the Kagera River in Burundi, which is the farthest headstream (a stream that is the source of a river) to flow into Lake Victoria. From the lake, the Nile proper heads north across eastern Africa for 4,132 miles to the Mediterranean. Its water is crucial to people living along its banks. They use it to irrigate precious crops, generate electricity, and, in the lower

## WORLD'S LONGEST RIVERS
Length in miles

Yellow River, China 3,395

Mississippi–Missouri river system, USA 3,710

Yangtze River, China 3,915

Amazon River, South America 4,000

Nile River, Africa 4,132

# WORLD'S TALLEST
# surf waves

Many of the world's tallest waves occur at Nazaré, Portugal. In November 2011, this is where veteran surfer Garrett McNamara from Hawaii rode a 78-foot-high monster wave to seize the world record—then a couple of years later he broke the world record again, at the same spot. The wave was estimated to be at least 100 feet high, but the measurement still must be confirmed.

# NAZARÉ,
## PORTUGAL

## WORLD'S TALLEST WAVES
Height in feet (year)

Nazaré, Portugal 100 (2013)

Caledonia Star, South Atlantic 98.43 (2001)

Lituya Bay, Alaska 98 (1958)

Nazaré, Portugal 78 (2011)

Draupner Oil Platform, Norway 60.7 (1995)

# WEATHER
# TRENDING #

## HEAVY WEATHER
### Falling stars

The National Weather Service tweeted a picture in January 2016 of some record-tying hail near Red Bluff, California. The hailstones, at three inches in diameter, were the largest to fall in the state in more than fifty years! It wasn't the size of the hailstones, however, that got people talking—the photograph, captured by storm-chaser Jeff Boyce, showed that the hailstones were unusually star-shaped.

## TWITTER DELUGE
### Most used weather hashtag

SaveOnEnergy studied 1.8 million tweets about the weather in 2016 to declare #flooding the most commonly used weather hashtag. An impressive 31 percent of the weather-related tweets in 2016 were about floods, compared to 15 percent about Hurricane Matthew, the runner-up. Other popular weather hashtags were #climate, #renewables, #drought, and #wildfires.

# SLAP!
Viral weather report

A 2016 video of a woman covering a storm in Barry, Wales, went viral worldwide after it showed her being knocked out by a surprise guest: a fish that flew through the air to hit her in the face. While the video was shared with a lot of laughter and enthusiasm, some naysayers claimed that the scene was staged, and that the fish looked like it had already been cleaned and gutted.

# BRIGHT AND BEAUTIFUL
Reddit's triple rainbow

One Reddit user set the content-sharing site abuzz in March 2016 after uploading a picture of a so-called "triple rainbow" from Oswego, New York. While the image racked up nearly a million views in a single day, some skeptics commented that it was likely not a true "triple rainbow,"—only five of which have been observed in the past 250 years, according to the Optical Society of America—but a reflection of the primary rainbow.

# RECORD SHAKERS
Year of the earthquake

Earthquakes made headlines again and again in 2016, causing some of the year's biggest natural disasters—like the Taiwan quake on February 6 and three earthquakes in as many months in central Italy. 2016 was a record-breaking year for seismic activity in New Zealand, which recorded almost 33,000 quakes, including one in November that registered a huge 7.8 on the Richter scale.

**incredible earth**

# COLDEST INHABITED PLACE
## on earth
# OYMYAKON

Extremely low air temperatures of −96.2°F in 1924 and −90°F in 1933 were recorded in the village of Oymyakon in eastern Russia, the lowest temperatures ever recorded in a permanently inhabited area. Only the Antarctic gets colder than this.

The five hundred people living in Oymyakon regularly experience temperatures below zero from September to May, with the December/January/February average falling well below −58°F. The town sits in a valley surrounded by snowy mountains.

## COLDEST PLACES ON EARTH

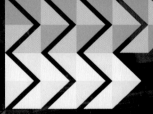

Coldest temperature recorded on Earth: Vostok Station, Antarctica −128.6°F

Coldest inhabited place on Earth: Oymyakon, eastern Russia −96.2°F

Coldest annual mean temperature: Resolute, Canada 3.7°F

# WORLD'S LARGEST ice sculpture
# ICE HOTEL

**OTHER ICE HOTELS**
SnowCastle of Kemi, Finland
Hôtel de Glace, Quebec City, Canada
Bjorli Ice Lodge, Norway
Hotel of Ice at Balea Lac, Romania
Ice Village, Shimukappu, Japan

Want to sleep on a bed made of ice in subzero temperatures? That is the prospect for guests at the world's largest ice sculpture—the original Icehotel and art exhibition in Jukkasjärvi, 125 miles north of the Arctic Circle in Sweden. Here, the walls, floors, and ceilings of the sixty-five rooms are made of ice from the local Torne River and snow from the surrounding land. The beds, chairs, and tables—and even the bar and the drinks glasses standing on it—are made from ice. A neighboring ice church hosts one hundred weddings each winter. The hotel is open from December to April, after which it melts back into the wild.

# MOST DEVASTATING
## wildfire of 2016
# FORT McMURRAY

On May 1, 2016, fire broke out in the forest southwest of Fort McMurray, Canada. It spread across 1,500,000 acres, destroyed 2,400 structures, and prompted the largest wildfire evacuation of people in Canada's history. Experts estimated that insurance claims might add up to C$4.7 billion or more, making this wildfire Canada's most costly disaster ever—higher than the 2011 Slave Lake fire and the 2013 Alberta floods.

## CALIFORNIA'S $229 MILLION FIRE

The Soberanes wildfire in California, USA, kept firefighters busy for almost three months in 2016. Having started in July, the fire ripped through 132,127 acres of wilderness before it was contained in mid-October.

# FORT MCMURRAY STATS

## 100–130

SPREAD OF FIRE AT ITS PEAK:
100–130 feet per minute

## 1,000

NUMBER OF FIREFIGHTERS
INVOLVED: 1,000 minimum

## 80,000

NUMBER OF RESIDENTS FORCED
TO FLEE: 80,000

## 10%

DAMAGE TO THE CITY:
10 percent destroyed

MOST INTENSE
## storm to hit land
# HAIYAN

Typhoon Haiyan is one of the most powerful storms ever recorded, and was the strongest-ever tropical storm to hit land. On November 8, 2013, it struck the Philippines, where it was known as Super Typhoon Yolanda.

Wind speeds reached 195 miles per hour and vast areas of the islands were damaged or destroyed. Around eleven million people were affected: Many were made homeless and at least 6,300 people were killed.

# AMERICA'S MOST costly tornado

# THE JOPLIN TORNADO

On May 22, 2011, a multiple-vortex tornado about one mile wide swept through Joplin, Missouri, killing 161 people and injuring more than one thousand others. It was the deadliest tornado in the United States since the 1947 Glazier-Higgins-Woodward tornadoes in which 181 people lost their lives. With $2.8 billion's worth of damage, the Joplin tornado was by far the costliest tornado in U.S. history. It was registered as an EF5 category tornado—the most intense kind—with winds in excess of 200 miles per hour. It ripped houses off their foundations and lifted cars and trucks into the air.

# HIGHEST TSUNAMI in the United States LITUYA BAY

On July 9, 1958, a severe 7.8 magnitude earthquake triggered a huge rockslide into the narrow inlet of Lituya Bay, Alaska. The sudden displacement of water caused a mega tsunami, with a crest estimated to be 98 feet high. The giant wave traveled across the bay and destroyed vegetation up to 1,722 feet above sea level. Five people died and nearby settlements, docks, and boats were badly damaged. It was the highest tsunami to be recorded in the United States in modern times.

# MOST DESTRUCTIVE
## storm surge in the
### United States

When Hurricane Katrina slammed into the Louisiana coast in 2005, a storm surge drove the sea almost 12.5 miles inland. New Orleans's hurricane surge protection was breached in fifty-three places, levees failed, boats and barges rammed buildings, and the city and countless neighboring communities were severely flooded. About 80 percent of New Orleans was underwater, close to 1,833 people lost their lives, and an area almost the size of the United Kingdom was devastated. The damage cost an estimated $108 billion. The U.S. Homeland Security secretary described the aftermath of the hurricane as "probably the worst catastrophe, or set of catastrophes" in the country's history.

# HURRICANE
# KATRINA

## MOST DESTRUCTIVE HURRICANES
## IN THE UNITED STATES
Wind speed in miles per hour

 **Labor Day Hurricane (1935) 185**

 **Hurricane Andrew (1992) 177**

 **Hurricane Katrina (2005) 175**

 **Galveston Hurricane (1900) 145**

# HOTTEST YEAR
## on record
### 2016

Data gathered by NASA's Goddard Institute for Space Studies shows that 2016 was the warmest year since records began in 1880. Global average temperatures were 1.78°F warmer than they were in the mid-twentieth century, and it was the third year in a row that global temperature records were broken, continuing a long-term warming trend. Most scientists agree that this temperature increase is caused by a rise in the greenhouse gas carbon dioxide and other human-made emissions in the atmosphere.

# MOST SNOWFALL
## in the United States

The most snowfall on record in the United States overall occurred at Tamarack, near the Bear Valley ski resort in California, on March 11, 1911. The snow reached an incredible 37.8 feet high. Tamarack also holds the record for the most snowfall in a single month, with 32.5 feet in January 1911. Mount Shasta, California, had the most snowfall in a single storm with 15.75 feet falling from February 13–19, 1959. The most snow in twenty-four hours was a snowfall of 6.3 feet at Silver Lake, Colorado, on April 14–15, 1921.

# CALIFORNIA
# AND
# COLORADO

## WORLD'S LARGEST
# hailstone
# VIVIAN, SOUTH, DAKOTA

In August 2010, the town of Vivian, South Dakota, was bombarded by some of the biggest hailstones ever to have fallen out of the sky. They went straight through roofs of houses, smashed car windshields, and stripped vegetation. Among them was a world record breaker, a hailstone the size of a volleyball. It was 8 inches in diameter and weighed 2.2 pounds.

# THE HUMAN
# lightning
# conductor

Roy Sullivan was a U.S. park ranger in Shenandoah National Park, Virginia. While going about his duties he was struck by lightning no fewer than seven times. He claimed he was also hit by lightning as a child, making a total of eight lightning strikes. It came to the point that whenever a faraway thunderstorm was heard approaching, his coworkers deliberately distanced themselves from him—just in case!

# ROY
# SULLIVAN

**8**

**state STATS**

STATE STATS
# TRENDING #

## BIG APPLE
### Instagram's most geotagged city of 2016

New York City was the most geotagged city in the world in 2016, according to Instagram. It came in ahead of London, England, in second place, and Moscow, Russia, in third. The popularity of the "Big Apple" on the app is no surprise, as the city is full of prime photo locations, such as Madison Square Garden, Brooklyn Bridge, Times Square, and Central Park—all of which made Instagram's list of the top twenty photo destinations for 2016.

## #ISTANDWITHSTANDINGROCK
### Showing support through Facebook check-ins

In 2016, Standing Rock, North Dakota, garnered national attention as protesters opposed the building of a new oil pipeline through Indian land. The proposed pipeline conflicted with the tribe's interest in protecting their land's cultural resources. The protest wasn't limited to those physically at the reservation, however—more than one million people around the country "checked in" at the location on Facebook in response to a viral post on October 30 that claimed the local sheriff's department was using social media check-ins to target people at the protest camp.

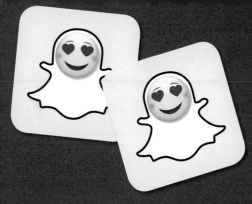

## CUTEST COUPLE
### Wisconsin's Snapchat love story

Love was in the air at the University of Wisconsin–Madison in April 2016, when "Mystery Girl" Abby Diamond replied to a Snapchat Campus Story featuring "Vikings Fan" Reed Bjork. The resulting interactions between the two went viral as they posted snaps, trying to coordinate meeting for the first time. The whole campus became invested in their growing love story, and the app even created a "help Vikings Fan find Mystery Girl" geofilter for the area.

## FRIENDS IN HIGH PLACES
### #BROTUS

The so-called "bromance" between President Barack Obama and Vice President Joe Biden went to a whole new level in August 2016, when Biden tweeted a picture of matching friendship bracelets with the pair's names for the president's birthday. His tweet, which read "Happy 55th, Barack! A brother to me, a best friend forever," got more than 335,000 retweets, becoming one of the vice president's most popular posts ever.

## HISTORY IN THE MAKING
### New national museum

The National Museum of African American History and Culture (NMAAHC) opened on the National Mall in Washington, DC, in September 2016—the museum's timed tickets were snapped up months in advance. The NMAAHC also launched a mobile app, designed by African American–owned tech firm Clearly Innovative, to complement its exhibits, allowing visitors to explore stories further and share them to their own social media accounts.

STATE WITH
THE OLDEST
# Mardi Gras
# celebration
# ALABAMA

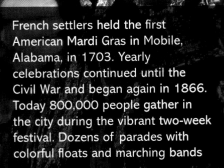

French settlers held the first American Mardi Gras in Mobile, Alabama, in 1703. Yearly celebrations continued until the Civil War and began again in 1866. Today 800,000 people gather in the city during the vibrant two-week festival. Dozens of parades with colorful floats and marching bands wind through the streets each day. Partygoers attend masked balls and other lively events sponsored by the city's social societies. On Mardi Gras, which means "Fat Tuesday" in French, six parades continue the party until the stroke of midnight, which marks the end of the year's festivities and the beginning of Lent.

# STATE WITH THE MOST
# pilots per capita
# ALASKA

Alaska is the only state in the United States in which more than 1 percent of citizens have a pilot's license—no surprise, considering Alaska has many islands, and is the largest and most sparsely populated state. If you think this means the state has a surplus of skilled aviators, think again: Despite having six times the national average of pilots per capita, newspapers reported in 2016 that a shortage in Alaska led the state to consider turning to drone technology. Many of its pilots and mechanics leave the state for high-flying careers in the lower forty-eight states.

## MOST PILOTS PER CAPITA
Number of pilots per 100 people

**Alaska 1.313**

**Montana 0.407**

**Colorado 0.393**

**North Dakota 0.383**

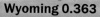

**Wyoming 0.363**

# STATE WITH THE BEST-PRESERVED
# meteor crater
# ARIZONA

Fifty thousand years ago, a meteor traveling at 26,000 miles per hour struck the Earth near present-day Winslow, Arizona, to create a mile-wide, 550-foot-deep crater. Today, Meteor Crater is a popular tourist destination, and is overseen by stewards who work to educate visitors about its formation. There is even an animated movie showing how it happened. The crater is sometimes known as the Barringer Crater, in recognition of mining engineer Daniel Moreau Barringer, who was the one to propose that it had been made by a meteorite. Previously, geologists had believed that the crater was a natural landform created over time.

# ONLY STATE WHERE
## diamonds
## are mined
# ARKANSAS

Crater of Diamonds, near Murfreesboro, Arkansas, is the only active commercial diamond mine in the United States. Farmer and former owner John Wesley Huddleston first discovered diamonds there in August 1906, and a diamond rush overwhelmed the area after he sold the property to a mining company. For a time, there were two competing mines in this area, but in 1969, General Earth Minerals bought both mines to run them as private tourist attractions. Since 1972, the land has been owned by the state of Arkansas, who designated the area as Crater of Diamonds State Park. Visitors can pay a fee to search through plowed fields in the hope of discovering a gem for themselves.

# ONLY STATE TO HOST
# the Summer and Winter Olympic games

California is the only state to have hosted both the Summer and Winter Olympics. Los Angeles hosted the Summer Games in 1932 and 1984, and Squaw Valley hosted the Winter Games in 1960. Squaw Valley is one of only three U.S. cities to have hosted the Winter Games—Lake Placid, New York, has hosted it twice, while Salt Lake City, Utah, hosted in 2002. Los Angeles is the only U.S. city to have hosted multiple Summer Games, and they have even made a bid to host the 2024 event. The only other cities in history to have hosted the Summer Olympics more than once are Paris, London, and Athens.

## HOSTS OF MULTIPLE OLYMPIC GAMES
### Number of Games hosted

Paris 3

London 3

Athens 2

Lake Placid 2

St. Moritz 2

## CALIFORNIA

# STATE WITH THE LARGEST
# elk population
# COLORADO

Colorado is currently home to around 276,000 elk, making it the state with the largest elk population. Elk live on both public and private land across the state, from the mountainous regions to lower terrain. Popular targets for hunting, these creatures are regulated by both the Colorado Parks and Wildlife department and the National Park Service. Many elk live within the boundaries of Colorado's Rocky Mountain National Park. Elk are among the largest members of the deer family, and the males—called bulls—are distinguishable by their majestic antlers.

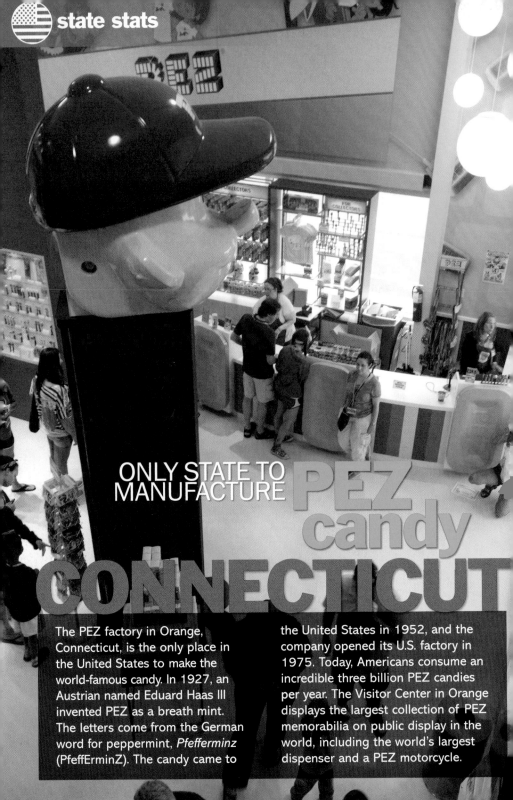

## ONLY STATE TO MANUFACTURE PEZ candy
# CONNECTICUT

The PEZ factory in Orange, Connecticut, is the only place in the United States to make the world-famous candy. In 1927, an Austrian named Eduard Haas III invented PEZ as a breath mint. The letters come from the German word for peppermint, *Pfefferminz* (PfeffErminZ). The candy came to the United States in 1952, and the company opened its U.S. factory in 1975. Today, Americans consume an incredible three billion PEZ candies per year. The Visitor Center in Orange displays the largest collection of PEZ memorabilia on public display in the world, including the world's largest dispenser and a PEZ motorcycle.

# STATE WITH THE MOST
# horseshoe crabs
# DELAWARE

Delaware Bay has the largest American horseshoe crab (*Limulus polyphemus*) population in the world. These crabs can be seen in large numbers on the bay's beaches in the spring. They appear during high tides on new and full moons, when they come onto land to spawn (deposit eggs). Horseshoe crabs—which are not actually related to other species of crab—have changed very little in the past 250 million years, and have therefore been called "living fossils." It is impossible to know the exact number of horseshoe crabs in the region, so every spring, volunteers at some of the state's beaches conduct counts to track spawning activity. In 2016, the Delaware Center for the Inland Bays reported a count of 15,418 horseshoe crabs across five beaches.

# STATE WITH THE MOST
## visited amusement park
# FLORIDA

Walt Disney World, in Lake Buena Vista, Florida, is home to several parks, including Magic Kingdom, the most visited amusement park in the United States. Disney World parks dominate the most-visited list, taking the top five spots. Magic Kingdom sees just over twenty million visitors from around the world who travel to Florida each year to ride the attractions, watch parades, and meet their favorite Disney characters. Divided into six themed areas, arguably the most iconic part of the park is Cinderella's Castle, which is illuminated each night by an impressive fireworks display and light-projection show.

## MOST VISITED AMUSEMENT PARKS
Number of visitors per year in millions

**Magic Kingdom, Walt Disney World, Florida 20.49**

**Disneyland, California 18.28**

**Epcot, Florida 11.8**

**Disney's Animal Kingdom, Florida 10.92**

**Disney's Hollywood Studios, Florida 10.83**

# Sports Hall of Fame
# GEORGIA

At 43,000 square feet, Georgia's Sports Hall of Fame honors the state's greatest sports stars and coaches. The museum includes 14,000 square feet of exhibition space and a 205-seat theater. It owns more than 3,000 artifacts and memorabilia from Georgia's professional, college, and amateur athletes. At least 1,000 of these artifacts are on display at any time. The Hall of Fame corridor features over 300 inductees, such as golf legend Bobby Jones, baseball hero Jackie Robinson, and Olympic track medalist Wyomia Tyus.

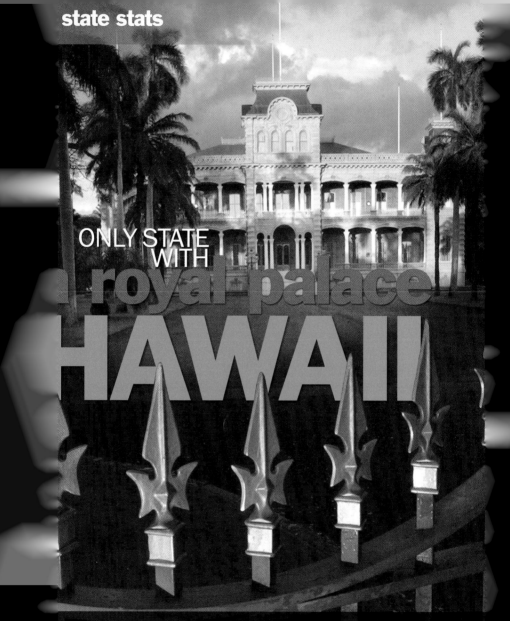

ONLY STATE
WITH
a royal palace
HAWAII

olani Palace, in downtown Honolulu, s the only official royal residence n the United States. The palace vas built from 1879–1882 by King Kalakaua, inspired by the styles of he grand castles of Europe. The monarchs did not live there for long, nowever: In 1893, the kingdom of Hawaii was overthrown by U.S. forces.

Kalakaua's sister, Queen Liliuokalani, was even held prisoner in the palace in 1895 following a plot to put her back on the throne. Iolani Palace was used as a government building until it became a National Historic Landmark in 1962. Restored to its nineteenth-century condition, it is now open to the public as a museum.

# ONLY STATE WITH a blue football field

Boise State's Albertsons Stadium, originally dubbed the "Smurf Turf" and now nicknamed "The Blue," is the only blue football field in the United States. In 1986, when the time came to upgrade the old turf, athletics director Gene Bleymaier realized that they would be spending a lot of money on the new field, yet most spectators wouldn't notice the difference. The solution came to Bleymaier while traveling on a plane: He would contact AstroTurf to create the new field in the school's colors. Since the field's creation, students at the school have consistently voted for blue turf each time the field has been upgraded. Today, Boise State's stadium is iconic in the world of college football, and has had visitors from all fifty states and thirty countries clamoring to see the field.

# IDAHO

# STATE WITH THE OLDEST
# free public zoo

Lincoln Park Zoo, in Chicago, Illinois, remains the oldest free public zoo in the United States. Founded in 1868—nine years after the Philadelphia Zoo, the country's oldest zoo overall—Lincoln Park Zoo does not charge admission fees. More than two-thirds of the money for the zoo's operating budget comes from food, retail, parking, and fundraising events. Nonetheless, the zoo continues to grow. In November 2016, it opened a new exhibit—the Walter Family Arctic Tundra—to house its newest addition: a seven-year-old male polar bear named Siku.

Kovler
LION HOUSE

ILLINOIS

# ONLY STATE WITH A SANTA CLAUS
# post office address

**INDIANA**

In 1856, the small town of Santa Fe, Indiana, changed its name to Santa Claus because the state already had a Santa Fe. The town's post office is the only one in the world with the Santa Claus name. The town is also home to the world's oldest Santa statue. The 22-foot figure was unveiled on December 25, 1935, and dedicated "to the children of the world." Every December a group of volunteers, including Santa's Elves Inc., answers some 13,000 letters that arrive in Santa Claus.

# state stats

## STATE WITH THE SHORTEST, STEEPEST
# railroad
# IOWA

At only 296 feet long, Fenelon Place Elevator in Dubuque, Iowa, is the shortest railroad in the United States, and its elevation of 189 feet also makes it the steepest. The original railway was built in 1882 by businessman and former mayor J. K. Graves, who lived at the top of the Mississippi River bluff and wanted a quicker commute down into the town below. Today's railway, modernized in 1977, is open to the public. It costs $1.50 for an adult one-way trip, and consists of two quaint house-shaped cars traveling in opposite directions on parallel tracks.

# STATE WITH THE MOST
## rock.
# concretions

Rock City, in Minneapolis, Kansas, boasts two hundred concretions of Dakota sandstone across a 5-acre park. They are the largest concretions in one place anywhere in the world. These concretions are huge spheres of rock, some of which measure up to 27 feet in diameter. They were created underground millions of years ago, when minerals deposited by water gradually formed hard, strong shells around small bits of matter in the sandstone. Over time, as the surrounding sandstone wore down, the concretions survived. Today, Rock City is a registered National Natural Landmark, and visitors can explore the park and climb the concretions for a $3.00 fee.

KANSAS

# KENTUCKY

## STATE WITH THE BIGGEST
# fireworks display

The Kentucky Derby is the longest-running sporting event in the United States and proudly claims to be the "most exciting two minutes in sport." It's also accompanied by the biggest fireworks display held annually in the United States: "Thunder Over Louisville," which kicks off the racing festivities. Zambelli Fireworks Internationale, who creates the display, says that the show requires nearly 60 tons of fireworks shells and a massive 700 miles of wire cable to sync the fireworks to music. The theme for the 2016 Thunder Over Louisville was "No Strings Attached."

# STATE WITH THE MOST
## crawfish
# LOUISIANA

The majority of the crawfish consumed in the United States are caught in the state of Louisiana. While these critters may look like tiny lobsters, crawfish are actually freshwater shellfish, and are abundant in the mud of the state's bayous—sometimes they are called "mudbugs." Before white settlers arrived in Louisiana, crawfish were a favorite food of the Native tribes, who caught them using reeds baited with venison. Today, crawfish are both commercially farmed and caught in their natural habitat. The industry yields between 120 and 150 million pounds of crawfish a year, and the crustaceans are an integral part of the state's culture, with backyard crawfish boils remaining a popular local tradition.

state with the oldest state fair

MAINE

SKOWHEGAN

STATE FAIR 1880

In January 1819, the Somerset Central Agricultural Society sponsored the first-ever Skowhegan State Fair. In the 1800s, state fairs were important places for farmers to gather and learn about new agricultural methods and equipment. After Maine became a state in 1820, the fair continued to grow in size and popularity, gaining its official name in 1842. Today, the Skowhegan State Fair welcomes more than 7,000 exhibitors and 100,000 visitors. Enthusiasts can watch events that include livestock competitions, tractor pulling, a demolition derby, and much more during the ten-day show.

# STATE WITH THE OLDEST
# capitol building
# MARYLAND

The Maryland State House in Annapolis is both the oldest capitol building in continuous legislative use and the only state house once to have been used as the national capitol. The Continental Congress met there from 1783–1784, and it was where George Washington formally resigned as commander in chief of the army following the American Revolution. The current building is the third to be erected on that site, and was actually incomplete when the Continental Congress met there in 1783, despite the cornerstone being laid in 1772. The interior of the house was finished in 1797, but not without tragedy—plasterer Thomas Dance fell to his death while working on the building's dome in 1793.

## OLDEST CAPITOL BUILDINGS IN 2016
Age of building (year work was started)

Maryland (1772) 244 years

Virginia (1785) 231 years

New Jersey (1792) 224 years

Massachusetts (1795) 221 years

New Hampshire (1816) 200 years

MASSACHUSETTS

STATE WITH
THE OLDEST
Thanksgiving
celebration

The first Thanksgiving celebration took place in 1621, in Plymouth, Massachusetts, when the Pilgrims held a feast to celebrate the harvest. They shared their meal with the native Wampanoag people from a nearby village. While the celebration became widespread in the Northeast in the late seventeenth century,

Thanksgiving was not celebrated nationally until 1863, when magazine editor Sarah Josepha Hale's writings convinced President Abraham Lincoln to make it a national holiday. Today, Plymouth, Massachusetts, holds a weekend-long celebration honoring its history: the America's Hometown Thanksgiving Celebration.

# MOST MAGICAL state

# MICHIGAN

Colon, Michigan, is known as the magic capital of the world. The small town is home to Abbott Magic Company—one of the biggest manufacturers of magic supplies in the United States—as well as an annual magic festival, magicians' walk of fame, and Colon Lakeside Cemetery, in which twenty-eight magicians are buried. The Abbott plant boasts 50,000 square feet dedicated to creating new tricks—from simple silk scarves to custom illusions. It is the only building in the world expressly built for the purpose of making magic.

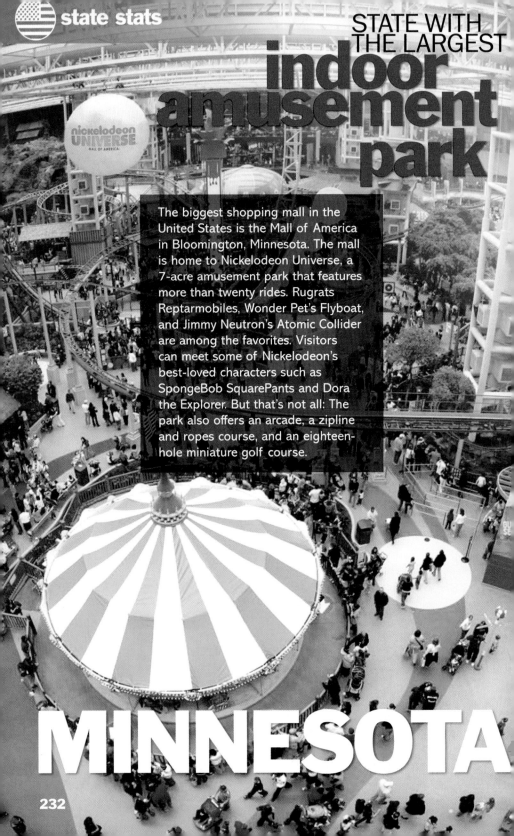

STATE WITH THE LARGEST

# indoor amusement park

The biggest shopping mall in the United States is the Mall of America in Bloomington, Minnesota. The mall is home to Nickelodeon Universe, a 7-acre amusement park that features more than twenty rides. Rugrats Reptarmobiles, Wonder Pet's Flyboat, and Jimmy Neutron's Atomic Collider are among the favorites. Visitors can meet some of Nickelodeon's best-loved characters such as SpongeBob SquarePants and Dora the Explorer. But that's not all: The park also offers an arcade, a zipline and ropes course, and an eighteen-hole miniature golf course.

# MINNESOTA

# MISSISSIPPI

## only state to hold the International Ballet Competition

Every four years, Jackson, Mississippi, hosts the International Ballet Competition, a two-week Olympic-style event that awards gold, silver, and bronze medals. The competition began in 1964 in Varna, Bulgaria, and rotated among the cities of Varna; Moscow, Russia; and Tokyo, Japan. In June 1979, the competition came to the United States for the first time, and, in 1982, Congress passed a Joint Resolution designating Jackson as the official home of the competition. In addition to medals, dancers vie for cash prizes and the chance to join established ballet companies.

# STATE WITH THE MOST popular underground wedding venue

# MISSOURI

It is no surprise that the "Cave State" is home to America's most popular underground wedding venue. More than three thousand couples have chosen to tie the knot at Bridal Cave in Camdenton, Missouri. Local lore says that the cave was discovered beneath Thunder Mountain centuries ago by Osage Indians and was the scene of a nineteenth-century wedding between Irona and her true love, Prince Buffalo. Considered one of the most scenic caves in the U.S., Bridal Cave is home to impressive stalagmites, a mysterious lake, and a record number of onyx formations, as well as the stalactite-adorned Bridal Chapel, which holds up to fifty guests.

# STATE WITH THE MOST
# T. rex specimens

The first *Tyrannosaurus rex* fossil ever found was discovered in Montana— paleontologist Barnum Brown excavated it in the Hell Creek Formation in 1902. Since then, many major *T. rex* finds have been in Montana—from the "Wankel Rex," discovered in 1988, to "Trix," discovered in 2013.

Another *T. rex* fossil was uncovered in Montana in 2016: "Tufts-Love Rex," named for paleontologists Jason Love and Luke Tufts, was found about 20 percent intact at the site in Hell Creek. Today, the Museum of the Rockies in Bozeman, Montana, houses thirteen *T. rex* specimens—more than anywhere else in the world.

# MONTANA

# STATE WITH THE LARGEST indoor rain forest

# NEBRASKA

The Lied Jungle at Henry Doorly Zoo in Omaha, Nebraska, features three rain-forest habitats: one each from South America, Africa, and Asia. At 123,000 square feet, this indoor rain forest is larger than two football fields. It measures 80 feet high, making it as tall as an eight-story building. The Lied Jungle opened in 1992 and cost $15 million to create.

Seven waterfalls rank among its spectacular features. Ninety different animal species live here, including saki monkeys, pygmy hippos, and many reptiles and birds. Exotic plant life includes the African sausage tree, the chocolate tree, and rare orchids. The zoo's other major exhibit—the Desert Dome—is the world's largest indoor desert.

# STATE THAT PRODUCES
# the most gold
# NEVADA

Although it has been called the "Silver State" for its silver production, Nevada is also the state that produces the most gold. According to the Nevada Mining Association, Nevada produces more than three-quarters of America's gold and accounts for 5.4 percent of world gold production. Gold can be found in every county of Nevada, although it is not always accessible to casual prospectors. Nevada's Carlin Trend is rich in gold deposits—and is, in fact, the world's second largest gold resource—but the deposits are so finely spread that they require an expensive process to extract the precious mineral.

# STATE WITH THE OLDEST skiing club

## NEW HAMPSHIRE

Nansen Ski Club, in Milan, New Hampshire, was founded by Norwegian immigrants in 1872, making it the oldest continuously operating skiing club in the United States. When it first opened, the venue only accepted other Scandinavians living in the area, but was then made available to everyone as more skiing enthusiasts began to move into New Hampshire from Quebec, to work in the mills there. For fifty years, the club was home to the largest ski jump east of the Mississippi, and was used for Olympic tryouts.

# STATE WITH THE MOST
# diners

## NEW JERSEY

The state of New Jersey has more than six hundred diners, earning it the title of "Diner Capital of the World." The state has a higher concentration of diners than anywhere else in the United States. They are such an iconic part of the state's identity that, in 2016, a New Jersey diners exhibit opened at Middlesex County Museum, showcasing the history of the diner from early twentieth-century lunch cars to modern roadside spots. The state has many different types of diners, including famous restaurant-style eateries like Tops in East Newark, as well as retro hole-in-the-wall diners with jukeboxes and faded booths.

# state stats

## STATE THAT MADE THE WORLD'S LARGEST
# flat enchilada

New Mexico was home to the world's largest flat enchilada in October 2014, during the Whole Enchilada Fiesta in Las Cruces. The record-breaking enchilada measured 10.5 feet in diameter, and required 250 pounds of masa dough, 175 pounds of cheese, 75 gallons of red chili sauce, 50 pounds of onions, and 175 gallons of oil. Led by Roberto's Mexican Restaurant, the making—and eating—of the giant enchilada was a tradition at the festival for thirty-four years before enchilada master Roberto Estrada hung up his apron in 2015.

## NEW MEXICO

# STATE WITH THE OLDEST state park

The Niagara Reservation was created in 1885, making Niagara Falls State Park the oldest state park in the country. Architect Frederick Law Olmsted and his fellow "Free Niagara" crusaders lobbied for fifteen years until the area was granted government protection against industrialists hoping to build there. The park consists of three waterfalls—American Falls, Bridal Veil Falls, and Horseshoe Falls—adding up to a total of 3,160 tons of water flowing over Niagara Falls every single second. Today, the park is more popular than ever, with summer 2016 seeing a record 103,000 visitors.

# NEW YORK

# STATE WITH THE LARGEST
## private house
# NORTH CAROLINA

The Biltmore Estate, in the mountains of Asheville, North Carolina, is home to Biltmore House, the largest privately owned house in the United States. George Vanderbilt commissioned the 250-room French Renaissance–style chateau in 1889, and opened it as a country retreat to his friends and family in 1895. Designed by architect Richard Morris Hunt, Biltmore House has an impressive thirty-five bedrooms and forty-three bathrooms, and boasts a floor space of over four acres. In 1930, the Vanderbilt family opened Biltmore House to the public.

## LARGEST PRIVATE ESTATES IN THE U.S.
Area in square feet

Biltmore Estate, Asheville, NC 175,000

Oheka Castle, Huntington, NY 109,000

Sydell Miller Mansion, Palm Beach, FL 84,626

Pensmore, Highlandville, MO 72,215

Rennert Mansion, Sagaponack, NY, 66,400

# STATE THAT GROWS THE MOST sunflowers
## NORTH DAKOTA

North Dakota grows more sunflowers than any other state in America, and half of the sunflowers produced nationwide. The state harvested 1.14 billion pounds of sunflowers in 2016, taking the crown from the next biggest producer, South Dakota, with 1.06 billion pounds. North Dakota grows two different types of sunflowers: confection flowers, which produce snacks such as sunflower seeds, and oil flowers, grown to produce sunflower oil. The flower crops in North Dakota may be huge, but not all the flowers survive. According to the United States Department of Agriculture, blackbirds damage five to ten million dollars' worth of sunflowers in North Dakota each year.

# STATE THAT MAKES ALL
# footballs used by the NFL

# OHIO

Since 1955, the Wilson Football Factory in Ada, Ohio, has been the sole manufacturer of footballs used by the National Football League. The company, which is the official partner of both the NFL and National Collegiate Athletic Association (NCAA) football, produces 700,000 balls a year—some feat, considering that each ball is laced by hand by Wilson employees and takes three days to make. Wilson proudly claims that every aspect of every ball is American made—the leather, for example, comes from Chicago—making the NFL the only major sports league in the country to use balls manufactured on home soil.

# STATE WITH THE LARGEST
# multiple-arch dam
# OKLAHOMA

Completed in 1940, the Pensacola Dam in Oklahoma is 6,565 feet long, making it the longest multiple-arch dam in the world. The dam stretches across the Grand River and controls the 43,500 acres of water that form the Grand Lake o' the Cherokees.

The massive structure is a towering 145 feet high and consists of no fewer than 535,000 cubic yards of concrete, about 655,000 barrels of cement, 75,000 pounds of copper, and a weighty 10 million pounds of structural steel.

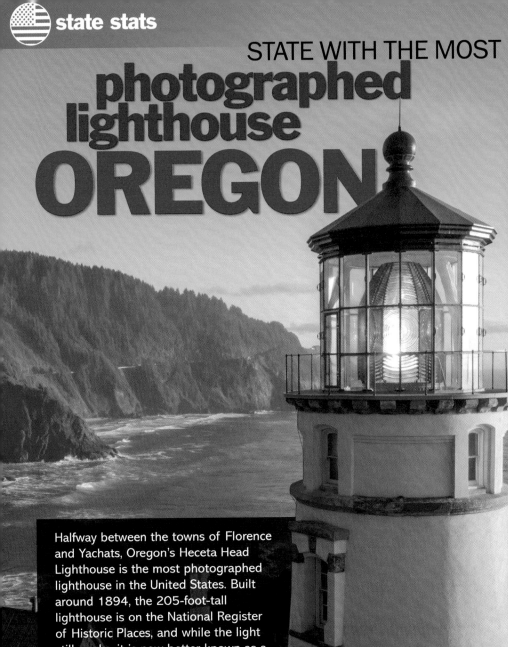

# STATE WITH THE MOST
# photographed
# lighthouse
# OREGON

Halfway between the towns of Florence and Yachats, Oregon's Heceta Head Lighthouse is the most photographed lighthouse in the United States. Built around 1894, the 205-foot-tall lighthouse is on the National Register of Historic Places, and while the light still works, it is now better known as a romantic bed-and-breakfast location. Heceta Head Lighthouse is famous not just for its beauty—it is also considered one of America's most haunted lighthouses, with stories claiming it is home to a "Gray Lady" called Rue.

# STATE THAT MANUFACTURES
# the most crayo

# PENNSYLVAN

Easton, Pennsylvania, is home to the Crayola crayon factory, and has been the company's headquarters since 1976. The factory produces an amazing twelve million crayons every single day, made from uncolored paraffin and pigment powder.

In 1996, the company opene Crayola Experience in downtc Easton. The Experience inclu live interactive show in which can watch a "crayonologist" crayons, just as they are mac factory nearby.

# STATE WITH THE OLDEST
# Fourth of July celebration

# RHODE ISLAND

Bristol, Rhode Island, holds America's longest continuously running Fourth of July celebration. The idea for the celebration came from Revolutionary War veteran Rev. Henry Wight, of Bristol's First Congregational Church, who organized "Patriotic Exercises" to honor the nation's founders and those who fought to establish the United States. Today, Bristol begins celebrating the holiday on June 14, and puts on a wide array of events leading up to the Fourth itself—including free concerts, a baseball game, a Fourth of July Ball, and a half marathon.

# STATE WITH THE HOTTEST pepper
## SOUTH CAROLINA

## WORLD'S HOTTEST PEPPERS
By peak heat in SHU

**Carolina Reaper 2,200,000**

**Trinidad Moruga Scorpion 2,009,231**

**7 Pot Douglah 1,853,936**

**7 Pot Primo 1,469,000**

**Trinidad Scorpion "Butch T" 1,463,700**

The Carolina Reaper, created by "Smokin" Ed Currie of Rock Hill, South Carolina, is officially the hottest pepper in the world, measuring an average of 1,569,300 Scoville heat units (SHU). Currie crossbred two other ultrahot peppers, a Pakistani Naga and a red habanero, to create the new champion. The ping-pong-ball-size pepper reportedly tastes deceptively sweet before the searing heat kicks in. Eating a Reaper is not for the faint of heart, but in 2016, New Yorker Wayne Algenio broke the world record by eating twenty-two Reapers in 60 seconds.

# STATE WITH THE LARGEST
# sculpture
# SOUTH DAKOTA

While South Dakota is famous as the home of Mount Rushmore, it is also the location of another giant mountain carving: the Crazy Horse Memorial. The mountain carving, which is still in progress, will be the largest sculpture in the world when it is completed, at 563 feet high and 641 feet long. Korczak Ziolkowski, who worked on Mount Rushmore, began the carving in 1948 to pay tribute to Crazy Horse—the Lakota Sioux leader who defeated General Custer at the Battle of the Little Bighorn. Nearly seventy years later, Ziolkowski's family continues his work, relying completely on funding from visitors and donors.

# STATE THAT MAKES ALL THE
# MoonPies
# TENNESSEE

Tennessee is the home of the MoonPie, which was conceived there in 1917 by bakery salesman Earl Mitchell Sr. after a group of local miners asked for a filling treat "as big as the moon." Made from marshmallow, graham crackers, and chocolate, the sandwich cookies were soon being mass-produced at Tennessee's Chattanooga Bakery, and MoonPie was registered as a trademark by the bakery in 1919. MoonPies first sold at just five cents each, and quickly became popular— even being named the official snack of NASCAR in the late nineties. Today, Chattanooga Bakery makes nearly a million MoonPies every day.

# STATE WITH THE OLDEST
# suspension bridge
# TEXAS

The Waco Suspension Bridge, which crosses the Brazos River in Texas, is the oldest bridge of its kind in the United States. When it opened in 1870, the 475-foot crossing was one of the longest single-span suspension bridges in the world. The bridge was originally owned by a private company that charged unpopular tolls to pay for the bridge's upkeep. In 1889, McLennan County purchased the bridge and then sold it to the City of Waco for just one dollar, after which it became toll free. Despite local calls to tear down the "unsightly" bridge in 1913, the City of Waco chose to refurbish and update it instead. Rightly so, since the structure is now on the National Register of Historic Places.

# STATE WITH THE LARGEST
# saltwater lake
# UTAH

Great Salt Lake, which inspired the name of Utah's largest city, is the largest saltwater lake in the United States, at around 75 miles long and 35 miles wide. Sometimes called "America's Dead Sea," it is typically larger than each of the states of Delaware and Rhode Island. Its size, however, fluctuates as water levels rise and fall: Since 1849, the water level has varied by as much as 20 feet, which can shift the shoreline by up to 15 miles. Great Salt Lake is too salty to support most aquatic life, but is home to several kinds of algae as well as the brine shrimp that feed on them.

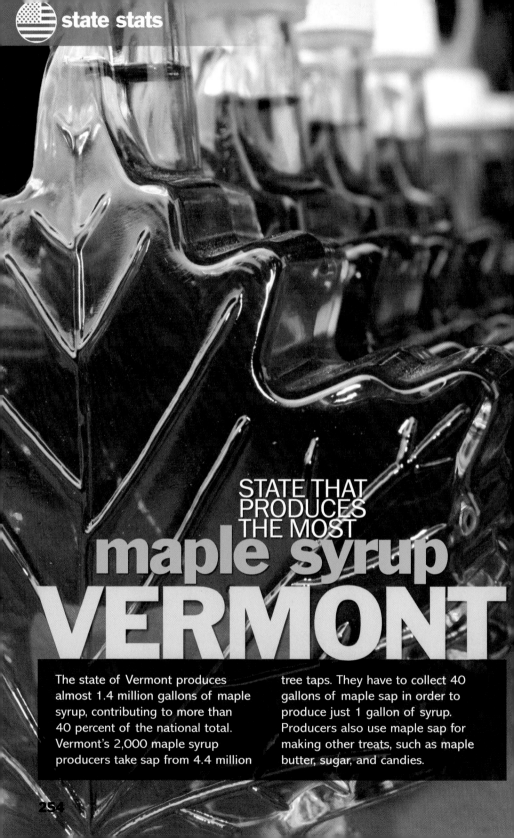

STATE THAT
PRODUCES
THE MOST
## maple syrup
# VERMONT

The state of Vermont produces almost 1.4 million gallons of maple syrup, contributing to more than 40 percent of the national total. Vermont's 2,000 maple syrup producers take sap from 4.4 million tree taps. They have to collect 40 gallons of maple sap in order to produce just 1 gallon of syrup. Producers also use maple sap for making other treats, such as maple butter, sugar, and candies.

# STATE WITH THE LARGEST
# office building
# VIRGINIA

The Pentagon—the headquarters of the United States Department of Defense—is America's largest office building. The five-sided structure, which was completed in 1943 after just sixteen months of work, cost $83 million to build. It contains 3.7 million square feet of office space— and triple the amount of floor space in the Empire State Building—as well as a large central courtyard. Despite containing 17.5 miles of corridors, the building's design means that a person can walk from any point to another in about 7 minutes. There are currently 24,000 employees, both military and civilian, working in the building.

# state stats

The Teapot Dome Service Station in Zillah, Washington, was once the oldest working gas station in the United States, and is still the only one built to commemorate a political scandal. Now preserved as a museum, the gas station was built in 1922 as a monument to the Teapot Dome Scandal, in which Albert Fall, secretary of the interior, took bribes to lease government oil reserves to private companies. The gas station, located on Washington's Old Highway 12, was moved in 1978 to make way for Interstate 82, then again in 2007 when it was purchased by the City of Zillah as a historic landmark.

STATE WITH
THE OLDEST
gas station
WASHINGTON

# STATE WITH THE LONGEST steel arch bridge

# WEST VIRGINIA

The New River Gorge Bridge in Fayetteville spans 3,030 feet and is 876 feet above the New River. It is both the longest and largest steel arch bridge in the United States. Builders used 88 million pounds of steel and concrete to construct it. The $37 million structure took three years to complete and opened on October 22, 1977. Bridge Day, held every October since 1980, is a BASE jumping event at the New River Gorge Bridge. Hundreds of BASE jumpers and some 80,000 spectators gather for the one-day festival. Among the most popular events is the Big Way, in which large groups of people jump off the bridge together. During Bridge Day 2013, Donald Cripps became one of the world's oldest BASE jumpers, at eighty-four years old.

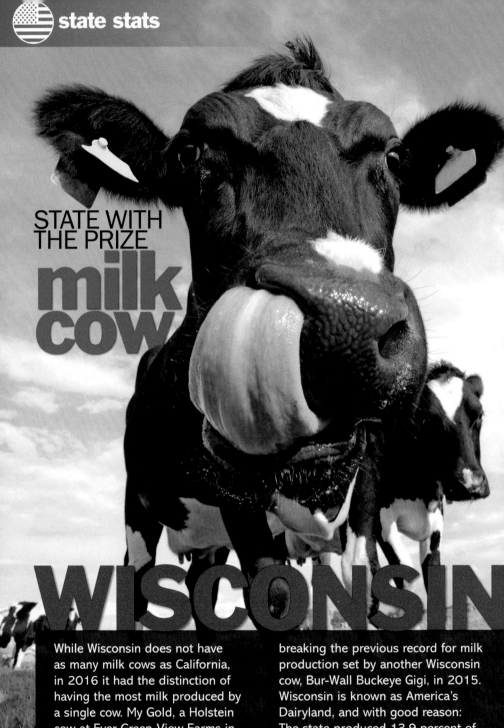

# STATE WITH THE PRIZE

# milk cow

# WISCONSIN

While Wisconsin does not have as many milk cows as California, in 2016 it had the distinction of having the most milk produced by a single cow. My Gold, a Holstein cow at Ever-Green-View Farms in Waldo, Wisconsin, produced nearly 77,500 pounds of milk in one year— breaking the previous record for milk production set by another Wisconsin cow, Bur-Wall Buckeye Gigi, in 2015. Wisconsin is known as America's Dairyland, and with good reason: The state produced 13.9 percent of the country's milk in 2016—30,123 million pounds in total.

# STATE WITH THE LARGEST
# hot spring
# WYOMING

Grand Prismatic Spring, in Yellowstone National Park in Wyoming, is the largest hot spring in the United States. The spring measures 370 feet in diameter and is more than 121 feet deep; Yellowstone National Park says that the spring is bigger than a football field and deeper than a ten-story building. Grand Prismatic is not just the largest spring but also the most photographed thermal feature in Yellowstone due to its bright colors. The colors come from different kinds of bacteria, living in each part of the spring, that thrive at various temperatures. As water comes up from the middle of the spring, it is too hot to support most bacterial life, but as the water spreads out to the edges of the spring, it cools in concentric circles.

sports
STARS

# SPORTS STARS
# TRENDING#↑

## #14STRONG
### Hockey world rallies around Denna Laing

Women's hockey player Denna Laing suffered a devastating spinal injury on New Year's Eve, 2015, during the National Women's Hockey League's first Outdoor Women's Classic game. Laing, however, impressed onlookers with her positive outlook following her injury. In 2016 there was an outpouring of support from the hockey community on social media as professional women's and college teams across the United States posted pictures of themselves spelling out the number fourteen—Laing's jersey number. Laing, who played for the NWHL's Boston Pride, was awarded the Dana Reeve Hope Award at the 2016 benefit gala for the Christopher and Dana Reeve Foundation in New York City.

## STEPH CURRY MVP
### Getting the vote

In May 2016, Golden State Warriors point guard Steph Curry trended on Twitter after he became the first player in NBA history to be unanimously voted as the league MVP (Most Valuable Player), receiving all 131 first-place votes from basketball reporters, broadcasters, and one fan. The accolade came after a historic season for Curry, when he became the first NBA player to average thirty points a game in less than thirty-five minutes per game over a full season.

## MAMBA OUT
### Kobe Bryant retires

Hashtags #MambaDay and #MambaOut trended on Twitter on April 14, 2016, following Kobe Bryant's retirement from professional basketball. Bryant, nicknamed the Black Mamba, ended his career with a marquee game, scoring sixty points in his final showing for the LA Lakers. After the game, Bryant was showered with purple and gold confetti as he gave a final speech to his fans, closing with the words, "Mamba out."

## KEEP POUNDING
### Top team hashtag

Professional sports teams all have their unique mottos—like the Alabama Crimson Tide's famous "Roll Tide" call, and "Dub Nation" for the Golden State Warriors. In the age of Twitter and Instagram, these mottos don't just adorn merchandise—they often become hashtags. According to Twitter, the most used team hashtag in 2016 belonged to the NFL's Carolina Panthers, with #KeepPounding. The motto honors late Panthers coach Sam Mills, who used the phrase in a 2004 speech and passed away in 2005.

## AMERICA'S PASTIME
### Most Instagrammed ballpark

Chicago's Wrigley Field beat out LA's Dodger Stadium as the most Instagrammed ballpark in the United States in 2016. The stadium's popularity was largely due to the success of the home team, the Chicago Cubs, who celebrated their centennial season at the park in 2016. Nicknamed the "Friendly Confines," Wrigley Field is known for its hand-operated scoreboard and for the white flag it flies after each game. The flag bears a blue "W" for a win and an "L" for a loss.

# FRED FUGEN AND VINCE REFFET

## HIGHEST base jump from a building

BASE jumping is just about the world's most terrifying sport to watch. BASE stands for the types of places a person may jump from: Buildings Antennae Spans (usually bridges) and Earth (usually cliffs). In April 2014, French daredevils Fred Fugen and Vince Reffet set a new record by jumping from a specially built platform at the top of the world's tallest building, the Burj Khalifa in Dubai. They jumped from a height of 2,716 feet, 6 inches. The highest ever BASE jump was performed by Russian Valery Rozov from 23,690 feet high on the north side of Mount Everest. He landed safely on the Rongbuk Glacier at an altitude of 19,520 feet, some 4,100 feet below.

# basketball shot

# How RIDICULOUS

Back in 2015, an Australian trick-shot team by the name of How Ridiculous scored from the top of the Gordon Dam in Tasmania to hit a long-range basket 415 feet below. A year later, American trick-shot stars Dude Perfect smashed this record, scoring a basket from 533 feet in Oklahoma. Not to be beaten,

How Ridiculous took the record once more, with a shot taken from the top of Mauvoisin Dam in Valais, Switzerland. As of November 2016, the record now stands at 593 feet and 9 inches. That's more than fifty stories!

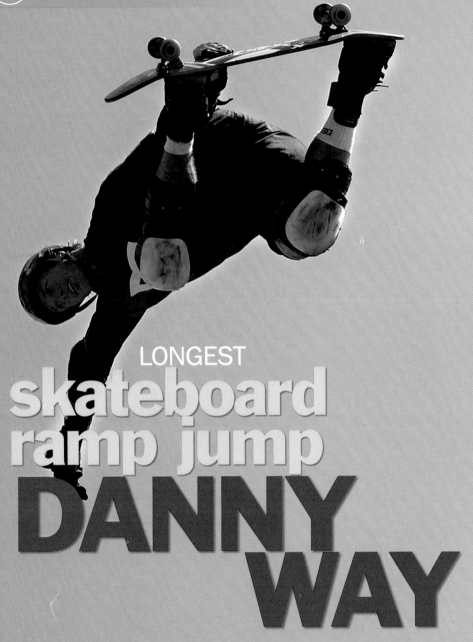

LONGEST
# skateboard
# ramp jump
# DANNY
# WAY

Many extreme sports activities are showcased at the annual X Games and Winter X Games. At the 2004 X Games, held in Los Angeles, skateboarder Danny Way set an amazing record that remains unbeaten. On June 19, Way made a long-distance jump of 79 feet, beating his own 2003 world record (75 feet). In 2005 he jumped over the Great Wall of China. He made the jump despite having torn ligaments in his ankle during a practice jump on the previous day.

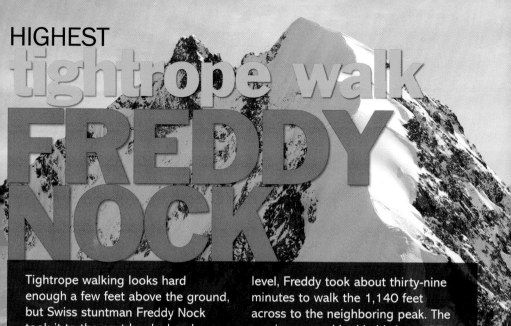

# HIGHEST
## tightrope walk
# FREDDY NOCK

Tightrope walking looks hard enough a few feet above the ground, but Swiss stuntman Freddy Nock took it to the next level when he walked between two mountains in the Swiss Alps in March 2015. On a rope set 11,590 feet above sea level, Freddy took about thirty-nine minutes to walk the 1,140 feet across to the neighboring peak. The previous record had held since 1974, when Frenchman Philippe Petit walked between the twin towers of New York's former World Trade Center.

HIGHEST-SCORING

# NBA game

# DETROIT PISTONS VS. DENVER NUGGETS

## 1983

The Detroit Pistons and the Denver Nuggets played this game in Denver on December 13, 1983. The game went to three overtime periods before the Pistons won 186–184, scoring 33 more points than the next-highest-scoring match (Spurs vs. Bucks, March 1982).

The Pistons' 186 points mark the highest total ever scored by a team. The losing team, Denver, also lost in the highest-scoring game without overtime: 162–158 points, won by the Golden State Warriors in November 1990.

## HIGHEST-SCORING NBA GAMES

Total points scored (final score)

| | |
|---|---|
| Detroit Pistons vs. Denver Nuggets | 370 (186–184) December 1983 |
| San Antonio Spurs vs. Milwaukee Bucks | 337 (171–166) March 1982 |
| Golden State Warriors vs. Denver Nuggets | 320 (162–158) November 1990 |
| Denver Nuggets vs. San Antonio Spurs | 318 (163–155) January 1984 |
| Phoenix Suns vs. New Jersey Nets | 318 (161–157) December 2006 |

# NBA team
## WITH THE MOST CHAMPIONSHIP TITLES
# BOSTON CELTICS

The Boston Celtics top the NBA winners' list with seventeen championship titles out of twenty-one appearances in the finals, just one title more than the Los Angeles Lakers. The two teams have met twelve times in the finals, resulting in nine wins for the Celtics. The best years for the Boston Celtics were the 1960s, with 1967 being the only year in the decade that they did not bring the championship home.

## NBA CHAMPIONSHIP WINS

| | | |
|---|---|---|
| Boston Celtics | 17 | 1957–2008 |
| LA Lakers | 16 | 1949–2010 |
| Chicago Bulls | 6 | 1991–1998 |
| San Antonio Spurs | 5 | 1999–2014 |
| Golden State Warriors | 4 | 1947–2015 |

# MOST CAREER POINTS
# in the NBA
# KAREEM ABDUL-JABBAR

Many fans regard Abdul-Jabbar as the greatest-ever basketball player. Abdul-Jabbar was known by his birth name, Lew Alcindor, until 1971, when he changed his name after converting to Islam. That same year he led the Milwaukee Bucks to the team's first NBA championship title. As well as being the all-time highest scorer of points during his professional career with a total of 38,387, Abdul-Jabbar also won the NBA Most Valuable Player (MVP) award a record six times.

## NBA MOST CAREER POINTS LEADERS
Number of points (career years)

| | |
|---|---|
| Kareem Abdul-Jabbar | 38,387 |
| Karl Malone | 36,928 |
| Kobe Bryant | 33,643 |
| Michael Jordan | 32,292 |
| Wilt Chamberlain | 31,419 |

On December 5, 2012, at thirty-four years and 104 days old, Kobe Bryant became the youngest player in NBA history to score 30,000 career points. This achievement was one of many highlights in Bryant's superb twenty-year pro career with the Los Angeles Lakers. Bryant helped lead the Lakers to five NBA Championships and was selected as an NBA All-Star eighteen times. By the time he retired in 2016, his points total had reached 33,643.

# YOUNGEST NBA PLAYER to reach 30,000 career points KOBE BRYANT

# WNBA PLAYER WITH THE MOST
## career points

TINA
THOMPSON

Tina Thompson was the number-one pick in the WNBA's first-ever draft in 1997. Joining the Houston Comets, she helped the team to win the championship in her rookie season. She played with the Comets until 2008 and then with the Los Angeles Sparks and Seattle Storm before retiring in 2013. Selected nine times as a WNBA All-Star, she also won two Olympic gold medals with the U.S. national team.

| MOST CAREER POINTS IN THE WNBA Number of points | |
|---|---|
| Tina Thompson | 7,488 |
| Tamika Catchings | 7,380 |
| Diana Taurasi | 7,311 |
| Katie Smith | 6,452 |
| Cappie Pondexter | 6,312 |

**272**

# WINNINGEST NCAA basketball coach ever

## PAT SUMMITT

Patricia "Pat" Summitt won 1,098 NCAA games as head coach of the University of Tennessee Lady Volunteers from 1974 to 2012, more than any other coach. Acclaimed as Naismith Coach of the Century in 2000, she also had a notable playing career, winning an Olympic silver medal as co-captain of the USA women's team in 1976.

When Summitt started coaching the Lady Vols in 1974, the first NCAA women's basketball championship was still eight years in the future. Her teams eventually won eight NCAA national titles, and in thirty-eight years as a coach, she never had a losing season. Ms. Summitt died of Alzheimer's disease in 2016, yet her impressive legacy lives on.

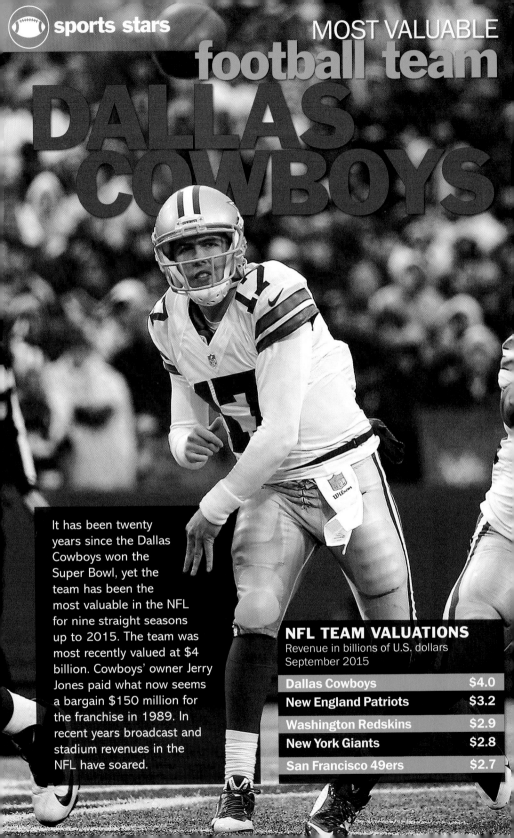

# MOST VALUABLE
## football team
# DALLAS
# COWBOYS

It has been twenty years since the Dallas Cowboys won the Super Bowl, yet the team has been the most valuable in the NFL for nine straight seasons up to 2015. The team was most recently valued at $4 billion. Cowboys' owner Jerry Jones paid what now seems a bargain $150 million for the franchise in 1989. In recent years broadcast and stadium revenues in the NFL have soared.

## NFL TEAM VALUATIONS
Revenue in billions of U.S. dollars
September 2015

|  |  |
|------|-------|
| **Dallas Cowboys** | **$4.0** |
| **New England Patriots** | **$3.2** |
| **Washington Redskins** | **$2.9** |
| **New York Giants** | **$2.8** |
| **San Francisco 49ers** | **$2.7** |

# NFL PLAYER WITH THE MOST
# career touchdowns
# JERRY RICE

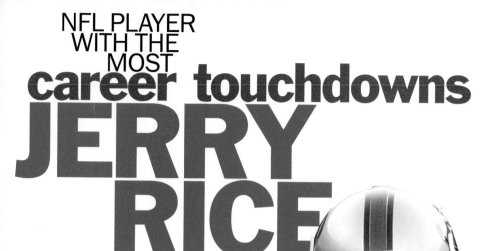

Jerry Rice is generally regarded as the greatest wide receiver in NFL history. He played in the NFL for twenty seasons—fifteen of them with the San Francisco 49ers—and won three Super Bowl rings. As well as leading the career touchdowns list with 208, Rice also holds the "most yards gained" mark with 22,895 yards. Most of his touchdowns were from pass receptions (197), often working with great 49ers quarterback Joe Montana.

## NFL PLAYERS WITH THE MOST CAREER TOUCHDOWNS
Number of touchdowns (career years)

| Player | Touchdowns | Career years |
| --- | --- | --- |
| Jerry Rice | 208 | 1985–2004 |
| Emmitt Smith | 175 | 1990–2004 |
| LaDainian Tomlinson | 162 | 2001–2011 |
| Terrell Owens | 156 | 1996–2010 |
| Randy Moss | 156 | 1998–2012 |

# NFL PLAYER WITH THE MOST
# pass completions
# BRETT FAVRE

## NFL PLAYERS WITH THE MOST PASS COMPLETIONS
Number of completions

| Brett Favre | 6,300 | 1991–2010 |
|---|---|---|
| Peyton Manning | 6,125 | 1988–2015 |
| Drew Brees | 5,836 | 2001– |
| Tom Brady | 5,244 | 2000– |
| Dan Marino | 4,967 | 1983–1999 |

After a handful of poor games as a rookie with the Atlanta Falcons, Brett Favre moved to the Green Bay Packers, then the New York Jets and the Minnesota Vikings. In eighteen of his twenty seasons with these teams, he passed for more than 3,000 yards. Favre, also known as "The Gunslinger," beat out all other NFL players for career passes completed. He also led the Packers to victory in Super Bowl XXXI, passing for two touchdowns and scoring a third himself.

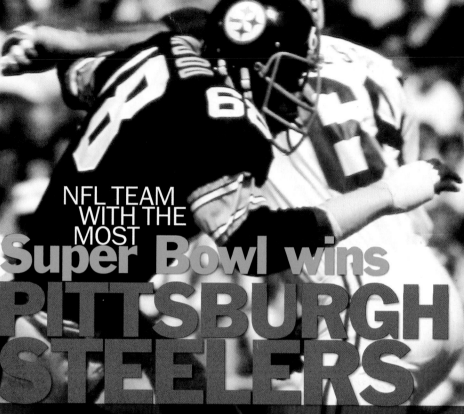

# NFL TEAM WITH THE MOST
# Super Bowl wins
# PITTSBURGH STEELERS

Although the Pittsburgh Steelers (founded in 1933 as the Pittsburgh Pirates) are one of the oldest pro-football teams, they were not very impressive in their early years. Since the 1970s, however, they have compiled one of the best all-around records in the NFL and now top the list with six Super Bowl wins out of eight appearances. The arrival of Chuck Noll as coach in 1969 was their turning point. Noll's teams, made up of such all-time greats as Terry Bradshaw, Franco Harris, and Joe Greene, won back-to-back Super Bowls twice.

## NFL TEAMS WITH THE MOST SUPER BOWL WINS
Number of wins

| Team | Number of wins | Super Bowls |
|------|----------------|-------------|
| Pittsburgh Steelers | 6 | Super Bowls IX, X, XIII, XIV, XL, XLIII |
| San Francisco 49ers | 5 | Super Bowls XVI, XIX, XXIII, XXIV, XXIX |
| Dallas Cowboys | 5 | Super Bowls VI, XII, XXVII, XXVIII, XXX |
| Green Bay Packers | 4 | Super Bowls I, II, XXXI, XLV |
| New York Giants | 4 | Super Bowls XXI, XXV, XLII, XLVI |
| New England Patriots | 4 | Super Bowls XXXVI, XXXVIII, XXXIX, XLIX |

# school with most Rose Bowl wins

The Rose Bowl is college football's oldest postseason event, first played in 1902. Taking place on or around January 1 of each year, the game is normally played between the Pac-12 Conference champion and the Big Ten Conference champion, but one year in three is part of college football's playoffs. The University of Southern California has easily the best record in the Rose Bowl, with twenty-five wins from thirty-four appearances, followed by the University of Michigan Wolverines (eight wins from twenty). The USC Trojans won the thrilling 2017 game, defeating the Penn State Nittany Lions 52–49 with a field goal in the final seconds.

# USC TROJANS

# MLB TEAM WITH THE MOST
# World Series wins

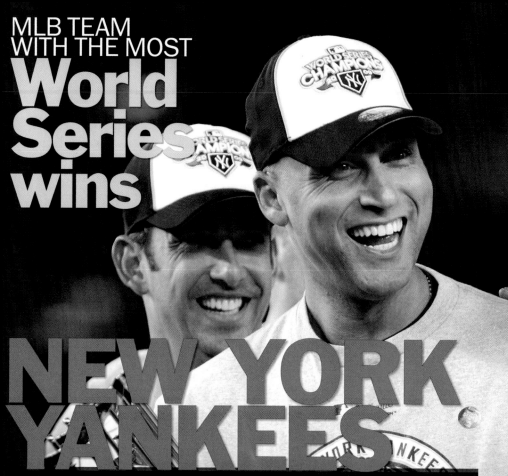

# NEW YORK YANKEES

## WORLD SERIES WINS
Number of wins

| New York Yankees | 27 | 1923–2009 |
|---|---|---|
| St. Louis Cardinals | 11 | 1926–2011 |
| Oakland Athletics* | 9 | 1910–1989 |
| San Francisco Giants** | 8 | 1905–2014 |
| Boston Red Sox*** | 8 | 1903–2013 |

\* Previously played in Kansas City and Philadelphia

\** Previously played in New York

\*** Originally Boston Americans

The New York Yankees are far and away the most successful team in World Series history. Since baseball's championship was first contested in 1903, the Yankees have appeared forty times and won on twenty-seven occasions. The Yankees' greatest years were from the 1930s through the 1950s, when the team was led by legends like Babe Ruth and Joe DiMaggio. Nearest challengers are the St. Louis Cardinals from the National League with eleven wins from nineteen appearances.

# MLB TEAM WITH THE HIGHEST
## salary LOS ANGELES DODGERS

Unlike some other sports, Major League Baseball has no team salary cap, and as revenues from television and other sources have increased in recent years player salaries have risen accordingly. For the 2016 season the Los Angeles Dodgers were yet again the highest-paying club, with a player salary bill of around $236.6 million. This included baseball's top earner, pitcher Clayton Kershaw, who earned $32.8 million. The Dodgers won the National League West Division in 2016 but were defeated by the resurgent Chicago Cubs in the World Series.

# LONGEST
# World Series
# championship drought

The 2016 World Series saw a dramatic showdown between the two Major League Baseball clubs with the longest World Series droughts: the Chicago Cubs and the Cleveland Indians. The Cubs had been one of baseball's most successful teams in the early years of the World Series at the start of the twentieth century, but between 1908 and 1945, they lost the World Series seven times. Following that string of World Series losses, the team scarcely won even a divisional title until 2016—the year the drought finally ended. The Cubs clinched the World Series title in the tenth inning in the deciding seventh game.

# CHICAGO CUBS,
# BROKEN 2016

## WORLD SERIES DROUGHTS

| Team | Last World Series win | Last appearance in World Series |
|------|----------------------|--------------------------------|
| Cleveland Indians | 1948 | 2016 |
| Texas Rangers | Never (since 1961*) | 2011 |
| Houston Astros | Never (since 1962*) | 2005 |
| Milwaukee Brewers | Never (since 1969*) | 1982 |
| San Diego Padres | Never (since 1969*) | 1998 |

* Dates when the teams were established.

sports stars

MLB PLAYER
WITH THE
HIGHEST
# batting
# average

## HIGHEST CAREER BATTING AVERAGES
Batting averages (career years)

| | | |
|---|---|---|
| Ty Cobb | .367 | 1905–1928 |
| Rogers Hornsby | .358 | 1915–1937 |
| Ed Delahanty | .346 | 1888–1903 |
| Tris Speaker | .345 | 1907–1928 |
| Ted Williams | .344 | 1939–1960 |

# TY COBB

Ty Cobb's batting average of .367 is one of the longest-lasting records in Major League Baseball. In reaching that mark, Cobb, known to fans as "The Georgia Peach," astonishingly batted .300 or better in twenty-three consecutive seasons, mainly with the Detroit Tigers. Cobb's status in the game was made clear when he easily topped the selection poll for the first set of inductees into the Baseball Hall of Fame.

## CAREER HOME RUNS
Number of home runs (career years)

| | | |
|---|---|---|
| Barry Bonds | 762 | 1986–2007 |
| Hank Aaron | 755 | 1954–1976 |
| Babe Ruth | 714 | 1914–1935 |
| Alex Rodriguez | 696 | 1994– |
| Willie Mays | 660 | 1951–1973 |

Barry Bonds's power hitting and skill in the outfield rank him as a five-tool player—someone with good speed and baserunning skills, who is also good at hitting the ball, fielding, and throwing. He played his first seven seasons with the Pittsburgh Pirates before moving to the San Francisco Giants for the next twelve seasons. He not only holds the record for most career home runs, but also for the single-season record of seventy-three home runs, which was set in 2001. Barry's godfather is Willie Mays, the first player ever to hit 300 career home runs and steal 300 bases.

# BARRY BONDS

## MLS PLAYER WITH THE MOST
# regular-season goals

# LANDON DONOVAN

Landon Donovan is Major League Soccer's all-time top scorer. After coming out of retirement for the 2016 season, Donovan now has 144 regular-season goals and 136 assists—again the record mark. In addition, Donovan holds the goal-scoring record for the U.S. national team, with 57 from 157 appearances. Donovan played for LA Galaxy for most of his career, but also appeared and scored in the German Bundesliga and the English Premier League.

## MLS REGULAR-SEASON TOP SCORERS
Number of goals (career years)

| | | |
|---|---|---|
| Landon Donovan | 144 | 2001– |
| Jeff Cunningham | 134 | 1998–2011 |
| Jaime Moreno | 133 | 1996–2010 |
| Chris Wondolowski | 121 | 2005– |
| Ante Razov | 114 | 1996–2009 |

# COUNTRY WITH THE MOST
# FIFA World
# Cup wins
# BRAZIL

Brazil, host of the 2014 FIFA World Cup, has lifted the trophy the most times in the tournament's history. Second on the list, Germany, has more runners-up and semifinal appearances and hence, arguably, a stronger record overall. However, many would say that Brazil's 1970 lineup, led by the incomparable Pelé, ranks as the finest team ever. The host team has won five of the twenty tournaments that have been completed to date.

## FIFA WORLD CUP WINNERS
Number of wins

| | | |
|---|---|---|
| Brazil | 5 | 1958, 1962, 1970, 1994, 2002 |
| Germany* | 4 | 1954, 1974, 1990, 2014 |
| Italy | 4 | 1934, 1938 1982, 2006 |
| Argentina | 2 | 1978, 1986 |
| Uruguay | 2 | 1930, 1950 |

Three teams have won the tournament once (England 1966, France 1988, Spain 2010).

* As West Germany 1954, 1974

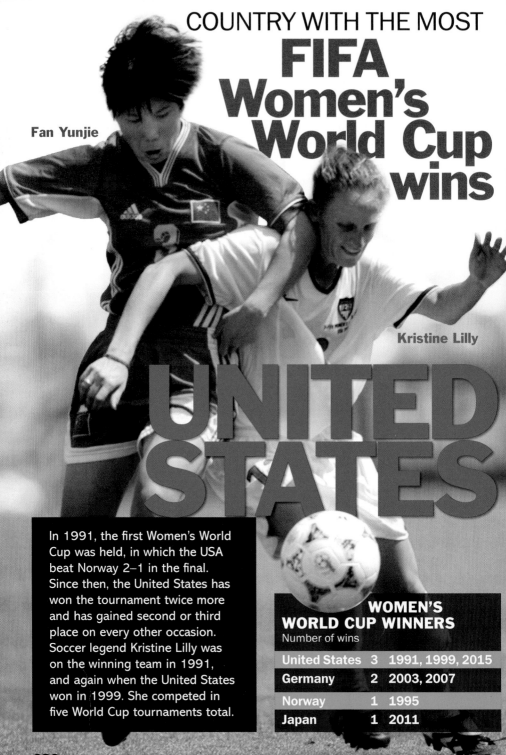

COUNTRY WITH THE MOST
# FIFA Women's World Cup wins

Fan Yunjie

Kristine Lilly

# UNITED STATES

In 1991, the first Women's World Cup was held, in which the USA beat Norway 2–1 in the final. Since then, the United States has won the tournament twice more and has gained second or third place on every other occasion. Soccer legend Kristine Lilly was on the winning team in 1991, and again when the United States won in 1999. She competed in five World Cup tournaments total.

## WOMEN'S WORLD CUP WINNERS
Number of wins

| | | |
|---|---|---|
| United States | 3 | 1991, 1999, 2015 |
| Germany | 2 | 2003, 2007 |
| Norway | 1 | 1995 |
| Japan | 1 | 2011 |

# KRISTINE LILLY

## WOMAN WITH THE MOST
## international soccer caps

In her long and successful career, Kristine Lilly has played her club soccer principally with the Boston Breakers. When she made her debut on the U.S. national team in 1987, however, she was still in high school. Her total of 354 international caps is the world's highest for a man or woman and her trophy haul includes two World Cup winner's medals and two Olympic golds.

## WOMEN WITH THE MOST INTERNATIONAL SOCCER CAPS
Number of caps (career years)

| | | |
|---|---|---|
| Kristine Lilly, USA | 354 | 1987–2010 |
| Christie Rampone, USA | 311 | 1997–2015 |
| Mia Hamm, USA | 276 | 1987–2004 |
| Julie Foudy, USA | 272 | 1988–2004 |
| Abby Wambach, USA | 255 | 2001–2015 |

# sports stars

## LOWEST WINNING SCORE
# in a major golf tournament

In Gee Chun of South Korea is still in the early stages of her professional career but has already achieved two wins in five annual women's golf "majors." Most remarkable of all was her achievement at the 2016 Evian Championship: the lowest score in a major championship by any player, male or female, at twenty-one under par. The previous women's record was nineteen under par, shared by five players, while two players share the men's record of twenty under par.

# IN GEE CHUN

# DUSTIN JOHNSON

## PGA GOLFER WITH LOWEST *season average*

South Carolina native Dustin Johnson had a great 2016 season, winning his first major, the U.S. Open, at Oakmont Country Club in June. He continued this success with impressive consistency, winning both of the 2016 season low-scoring titles for the PGA Tour: the Vardon Trophy and the Byron Nelson Award. He also topped the 2016 money list, winning over $9.6 million. Johnson has won at least one tournament every year since he joined the PGA Tour in 2008, currently the record winning streak.

# WOMAN WITH THE MOST
## Grand Slam titles
# MARGARET COURT

The Grand Slam tournaments are the four most important tennis events of the year: the Australian Open; the French Open; Wimbledon; and the U.S. Open. The dominant force in women's tennis throughout the 1960s and into the 1970s, Australia's Margaret Court heads the all-time singles list with twenty-four, although Serena Williams is catching up fast. Court won an amazing sixty-four Grand Slam titles in singles, women's doubles, and mixed doubles, a total that seems unlikely to be beaten.

## TOTAL GRAND SLAM TITLES
Number of singles titles (years active)

| | | |
|---|---|---|
| Margaret Court, Australia | 64 (24) | 1960–1975 |
| Martina Navratilova, Czech/USA | 59 (18) | 1974–2006 |
| Serena Williams, USA | 39 (23) | 1998– |
| Billie Jean King, USA | 39 (12) | 1961–1980 |
| Margaret Osborne duPont, USA | 37 (6) | 1941–1962 |

# MAN WITH THE MOST
# Grand Slam titles
# ROGER FEDERER

With eighteen wins, Swiss tennis star Roger Federer stands at the top of the all-time rankings in Grand Slam tennis singles tournaments. His best tournament has been Wimbledon, which he has won seven times. Federer did not win a Grand Slam between 2012 and 2016, but was a runner-up once in 2014 and twice in 2015. He missed the 2016 French Open due to a back injury, which ended his run of sixty-five consecutive Grand Slam appearances.

## GRAND SLAM SINGLES WINS
Number of wins (years active)

| | | |
|---|---|---|
| Roger Federer, Switzerland | 18 | 1998– |
| Rafael Nadal, Spain | 14 | 2001– |
| Pete Sampras, USA | 14 | 1988–2002 |
| Roy Emerson, Australia | 12 | 1961–1973 |
| Novak Djokovic, Serbia | 12 | 2003– |

# HIGHEST-PAID
# NASCAR driver
# JIMMIE JOHNSON

From a hobby that started on a 50cc motorcycle at age five, Californian racing driver Jimmie Johnson—now forty-one—was NASCAR's highest-paid driver of 2016 with an income of $21.8 million. Not far behind him, with $21.1 million, Dale Earnhardt Jr. has held the top spot for the last eight years. The news came as Johnson won the NASCAR Cup Series for the seventh time following a victory at the final race of the season. Johnson's NASCAR winnings are bolstered through sponsorship deals with Blue Bunny, Chevrolet, Gatorade, and Seiko.

## HIGHEST-PAID NASCAR DRIVERS 2016
In millions of U.S. dollars

| $21.8 | $21.1 | $15.2 | $15 | $13.9 |
|-------|-------|-------|-----|-------|
| Jimmie Johnson | Dale Earnhardt Jr. | Denny Hamlin | Kyle Busch | Kevin Harvick |

# Triple Crown wins

# EDDIE ARCARO

Many horse-racing experts think that Eddie Arcaro was the best-ever American jockey. Arcaro rode his first winner in 1932, and by the time of his retirement thirty years later, he had won the Triple Crown twice, in 1941 and 1948. He also won more Triple Crown races than any other jockey, although Bill Hartack has equaled Arcaro's total of five successes in the Kentucky Derby. Arcaro won 4,779 races overall in his career.

## JOCKEYS WITH MULTIPLE WINS IN TRIPLE CROWN RACES
Number of wins

| | | |
|---|---|---|
| Eddie Arcaro | 17 | 1938–1957 |
| Bill Shoemaker | 11 | 1955–1986 |
| Earl Sande | 9 | 1921–1930 |
| Bill Hartack | 9 | 1956–1969 |
| Pat Day | 9 | 1985–2000 |
| Gary Stevens | 9 | 1988–2013 |

# NHL TEAM WITH THE MOST
# Stanley Cup
# wins

The Montreal Canadiens are the oldest and, by far, the most successful National Hockey League team. In its earliest years, the Stanley Cup had various formats, but since 1927, it has been awarded exclusively to the champion NHL team—and the Canadiens have won it roughly one year in every four. The most successful years were the 1940s through the 1970s, when the team was inspired by all-time greats like Maurice Richard and Guy Lafleur.

## STANLEY CUP WINNERS (SINCE 1915)
Number of wins

| Team | Wins | Years |
|---|---|---|
| Montreal Canadiens | 24 | 1916–1993 |
| Toronto Maple Leafs | 11 | 1918–1967 |
| Detroit Red Wings | 11 | 1936–2008 |
| Boston Bruins | 6 | 1929–2011 |
| Chicago Blackhawks | 6 | 1934–2015 |

# MONTREAL CANADIENS

# JONATHAN TOEWS

## HIGHEST-PAID
## NHL
## player

The Chicago Blackhawks' Jonathan Toews was the NHL's highest-paid player for the 2016–17 season—between salary and endorsements, Toews earned a reported total of $16 million. In 2014, Toews and teammate Patrick Kane signed matching deals with the Blackhawks earning them each $84 million over eight years. Toews was the Blackhawks' youngest-ever team captain when appointed in 2008, and has since led the team to three Stanley Cup wins in six years, including the Blackhawks' first win since 1961. Toews is the youngest member of the "triple gold club," having won a Stanley Cup, World Championship gold, and an Olympic gold medal by age twenty-two. Only twenty-seven players in history have achieved all three victories.

# NHL PLAYER WITH THE MOST
# career points

# WAYNE GRETZKY

Often called "The Great One," Wayne Gretzky is regarded as the finest-ever hockey player. As well as scoring more goals and assists than any other NHL player—both in regular-season and in postseason games—Gretzky held over sixty NHL records in all by the time of his retirement in 1999. The majority of these records still stand. Although he was unusually small for an NHL player, Gretzky had great skills and an uncanny ability to be in the right place at the right time.

## NHL ALL-TIME HIGHEST REGULAR-SEASON SCORERS
Number of points (including goals) (career years)

| | | |
|---|---|---|
| Wayne Gretzky | 2,857 (894) | 1978–1999 |
| Mark Messier | 1,887 (694) | 1979–2004 |
| Jaromír Jágr | 1,868 (749) | 1990– |
| Gordie Howe | 1,850 (801) | 1946–1979 |
| Ron Francis | 1,798 (549) | 1981–2004 |

# CONNOR
# MCDAVID

At nineteen years old, center Connor McDavid was named team captain of the Edmonton Oilers at the beginning of the 2016–17 season. Remarkably, the season before that was his first in the NHL—and he missed a large part of it because of injury. McDavid, who has been hailed as the "Next One" (hockey's next household name), was drafted first overall in the NHL in 2015 after a stellar career in junior and age-group competitions.

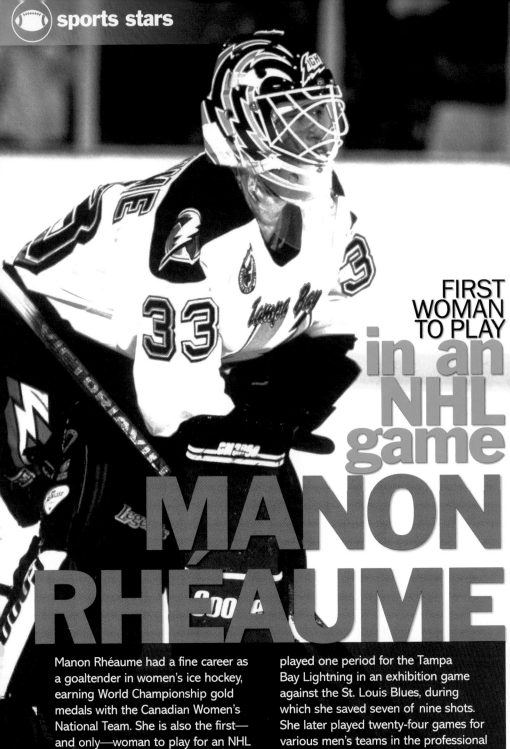

FIRST
WOMAN
TO PLAY
# in an
# NHL
# game
# MANON
# RHÉAUME

Manon Rhéaume had a fine career as a goaltender in women's ice hockey, earning World Championship gold medals with the Canadian Women's National Team. She is also the first— and only—woman to play for an NHL club. On September 23, 1992, she played one period for the Tampa Bay Lightning in an exhibition game against the St. Louis Blues, during which she saved seven of nine shots. She later played twenty-four games for various men's teams in the professional International Hockey League.

# FASTEST
# spin
# on ice
# skates

# OLIVIA RYBICKA-OLIVER

Although only eleven years old at the time of her record-breaking performance, Olivia Rybicka-Oliver from Nova Scotia, Canada, achieved an astonishing spin rate of 342 revolutions per minute—over five per second. This smashed the previous record of 308 revolutions per minute.

Olivia, who is Polish by birth, set her record in Warsaw on January 19, 2015. Her performance was part of a fund-raising event held by Poland's Fundacja Dziecięca Fantazja (Children's Fantasy Foundation) for terminally ill children.

Jamaica's Usain Bolt is the greatest track sprinter who has ever lived. Other brilliant Olympic finalists have described how all they can do is watch as he almost disappears into the distance. Usain's greatest victories have been his triple Olympic gold medals at Beijing 2008, London 2012, and Rio 2016. He holds the 100 meter world record (9.58s) and the 200 meter record (19.19s), both from the 2009 World Championships.

# FASTEST
## man in the world
# USAIN BOLT

## FASTEST 100-METER SPRINTS OF ALL TIME
Time in seconds

Usain Bolt (Jamaica) 9.58 Berlin 2009

Usain Bolt (Jamaica) 9.63 London 2012

Usain Bolt (Jamaica) 9.69 Beijing 2008

Tyson Gay (USA) 9.69 Shanghai 2009

Yohan Blake (Jamaica) 9.69 Lausanne 2012

## MOST MEDALS
# won by a nation in one Summer Olympics
# USA

The record medal count of 239 (including 78 golds) has been held by the United States since the 1904 Games in St. Louis, Missouri. In those days, international travel was much more difficult than it is now—as a result, it's estimated that about 90 percent of the competitors were Americans! Just twelve countries competed and only ten countries won any medals. By comparison, 206 countries competed at Rio 2016.

# MOST MEDALS
# won by an individual

# MICHAEL PHELPS

Michael Phelps may be the greatest competitive swimmer ever. He did not win any medals at his first Olympics in 2000, but at each of the Summer Games from 2004 through 2016 he was the most successful individual athlete of any nation. When he announced his retirement after London 2012, he was already the most decorated Olympic athlete ever—but he didn't stay retired for long. At Rio 2016 he won five more golds and a silver, taking his medal total to twenty-eight—twenty-three of them gold.

## MOST SUCCESSFUL OLYMPIANS
Number of medals won (gold)

| Name | Country | Sport | Years | Medals |
|------|---------|-------|-------|--------|
| Michael Phelps | USA | Swimming | 2004–16 | 28 (23) |
| Larisa Latynina | USSR | Gymnastics | 1956–64 | 18 (9) |
| Nikolai Andrianov | USSR | Gymnastics | 1972–80 | 15 (7) |

Four athletes, Ole Einar Bjørndalen of Norway, Boris Shakhlin of the Soviet Union, Edoardo Mangiarotti of Italy, and Takashi Ono of Japan, have each won thirteen medals.

# MOST DECORATED
# American gymnast ever

Although she was only nineteen during the Rio Olympics, Simone Biles's four gold medals and one bronze took her medal tally from world championships and Olympics to nineteen, a new American record. Biles is only four foot eight, but her tiny frame is full of power and grace, displayed most memorably in her favorite floor exercise discipline. Perhaps the only glitch in her career so far was when a bee chased her off the podium when she was being awarded her 2014 World All-Around gold medal.

## SIMONE BILES

Rio2016

# FIRST OLYMPIC GAMES
# to feature a refugee team

At the 2016 Rio Summer Games, ten athletes competed as members of the world's first Olympic Refugee Team. Over two hundred traditional countries have competed at the Olympics since 1896. According to the International Olympic Committee, the inclusion of a refugee team in 2016 was "an important signal to the international community that refugees are our fellow human beings and an enrichment to society." The ten athletes competed in track and marathon running, swimming, and judo. Five were originally from South Sudan, the world's newest country.

## RIO 2016

# MOST DECORATED
## Paralympian ever
# TRISCHA ZORN

Trischa Zorn is the most successful Paralympian of all time, having won an astonishing fifty-five medals, forty-one of them gold, at the Paralympic Games from 1980 to 2000. She won every Paralympic event she entered from 1980 to 1988. Zorn is blind and helps disabled military veterans enter the world of parasport. Zorn was inducted into the Paralympic Hall of Fame in 2012.

**LEADING FEMALE PARALYMPIC MEDALISTS**
Number of medals won

Trischa Zorn, USA 55
Beatrice Hess, France 25
Sarah Storey, Great Britain 25
Chantal Petitclerc, Canada 21
Mayumi Narita, Japan 20

# COUNTRY WITH THE MOST
# all-time Paralympic
# medals
USA

Although China topped the Paralympic medal table at the 2016 Summer Games in Rio (239 medals), with the United States coming in fourth (115 medals), the United States comfortably leads the all-time medal count in the Paralympic Summer Games. Norway heads the standings in the Winter Games, with the United States in third, giving the United States an overall medal total that will be unbeatable for many years to come.

## COUNTRY WITH THE MOST PARALYMPIC MEDALS
Total number of medals won

| | |
|---|---|
| United States | 2,458 |
| Great Britain | 1,817 |
| Canada | 1,192 |
| France | 1,189 |
| China | 1,022 |

# FIRST
# Paralympic
# triathlon

## RIO 2016

Most people would find a 750-meter swim, followed by a 20-kilometer bike ride, then a 5-kilometer run quite challenging—but then try all that with a physical or visual impairment, too. That's how it is for paratriathletes. Sixty Paralympians qualified for the first-ever Olympic paratriathlon at Rio in 2016. Only six of the possible ten events (men and women) were contested in Rio, with the United States' two golds, one silver, and one bronze being the best national result.

# index

# Photo credits

SCHOLASTIC
SUMMER
READING
CHALLENGE™

SCHOLASTIC.COM/SUMMER

# HAPPY CAMPER

## Take a Reading Adventure

The 2017 Scholastic Summer Reading Challenge was one for the books! This summer, Scholastic challenged students from around the world to read a little bit every day, just for fun. Those reading minutes added up quickly, and this year's numbers proved it! From May 8 to September 8, 2017, students from the U.S. and around the world read a whopping total of **138,399,392 minutes**! That's the fifth year in a row kids logged more than 100 million minutes. WOW!

## CONGRATULATIONS TO ALL STUDENTS WHO PARTICIPATED IN 2017!

## STUDENTS FROM AROUND THE WORLD PARTICIPATED!

Schools from 14 countries and two US territories added minutes to the Scholastic Summer Reading Challenge. Three international schools read more than 100,000 minutes, led by Greenoak International School in Port Harcourt, Nigeria, with **690,938 minutes**, and Seoul Foreign School in Seoul, South Korea, with **352,704 minutes**. Top countries and territories include:

| | |
|---|---|
| Bahamas | South Korea |
| Canada | Spain |
| China | Taiwan |
| Colombia | Thailand |
| Nigeria | United Arab Emirates |
| Puerto Rico | US Virgin Islands |

## STATES WITH THE MOST MINUTES READ
### Did your state make the top 20?

| Number of participating schools: | Total number of students who logged minutes: | Number of schools logging 100,000 minutes or more: |
|---|---|---|
| **3,556** | **184,214** | **238** |

## TOP 20 STATES WITH THE MOST MINUTES READ:

| | | |
|---|---|---|
| 1. | Texas | 28,468,135 |
| 2. | Florida | 10,087,366 |
| 3. | Pennsylvania | 7,967,560 |
| 4. | Louisiana | 7,782,666 |
| 5. | Massachusetts | 7,275,762 |
| 6. | Georgia | 6,695,086 |
| 7. | New York | 5,077,265 |
| 8. | New Jersey | 4,992,159 |
| 9. | North Carolina | 4,744,693 |
| 10. | Michigan | 4,415,881 |
| 11. | California | 4,317,948 |
| 12. | Arizona | 2,715,381 |
| 13. | Rhode Island | 2,202,408 |
| 14. | Virginia | 2,081,028 |
| 15. | Colorado | 1,888,469 |
| 16. | Tennessee | 1,705,885 |
| 17. | Ohio | 1,689,983 |
| 18. | Kentucky | 1,656,070 |
| 19. | Illinois | 1,630,669 |
| 20. | Maryland | 1,405,586 |

# "BEST IN STATE" SCHOOLS

These schools all earned top honors by reading the most in their state.

| State | School | City | Minutes |
|---|---|---|---|
| Alabama | Williams Intermediate School | Pell City | 971,925 |
| Alaska | Sand Lake Elementary School | Anchorage | 92,954 |
| Arizona | American Leadership Academy-Anthem | Florence | 1,211,877 |
| Arkansas | The New School | Fayetteville | 263,312 |
| California | Hirsch Elementary School | Fremont | 1,200,096 |
| Colorado | Prospect Ridge Academy | Broomfield | 338,915 |
| Connecticut | Scotland Elementary School | Scotland | 270,206 |
| Delaware | Las Americas Aspira Academy | Newark | 296,341 |
| District of Columbia | Holy Trinity School | Washington | 26,405 |
| Florida | New River Elementary School | Wesley Chapel | 5,380,415 |
| Georgia | Dodgen Middle School | Marietta | 713,425 |
| Hawaii | Laie Elementary School | Laie | 174,303 |
| Idaho | Peregrine Elementary School | Meridian | 1,111,959 |
| Illinois | Walnut Trails Elementary School | Shorewood | 281,736 |
| Indiana | Allisonville Elementary School | Indianapolis | 381,807 |
| Iowa | Resurrection School | Dubuque | 192,447 |
| Kansas | St. Thomas Aquinas School | Wichita | 356,719 |
| Kentucky | Lowe Elementary School | Louisville | 633,281 |
| Louisiana | Lisa Park Elementary School | Houma | 6,101,119 |
| Maine | Brewer Community School | Brewer | 390,481 |
| Maryland | Bradley Hills Elementary School | Bethesda | 535,498 |
| Massachusetts | James M. Quinn Elementary School | North Dartmouth | 946,163 |
| Michigan | Daisy Brook Elementary School | Fremont | 1,687,149 |
| Minnesota | Maranatha Christian Academy | Brooklyn Park | 497,566 |
| Mississippi | Annunciation Catholic School | Columbus | 672,794 |
| Missouri | Spoede Elementary School | Saint Louis | 191,466 |
| Montana | Roosevelt Elementary School | Great Falls | 140,326 |
| Nebraska | West Dodge Station Elementary School | Elkhorn | 592,289 |
| Nevada | Coral Academy Science | Las Vegas | 5,894 |
| New Hampshire | Rochester Middle School | Rochester | 308,234 |
| New Jersey | Newell Elementary School | Allentown | 1,582,783 |
| New Mexico | University Hills Elementary School | Las Cruces | 488,193 |
| New York | Village Elementary School | Hilton | 996,027 |
| North Carolina | Ballantyne Elementary School | Charlotte | 876,114 |
| North Dakota | Erik Ramstad Middle School | Minot | 762,773 |
| Ohio | Mulberry Elementary School | Milford | 263,788 |
| Oklahoma | Northeast Elementary School | Owasso | 218,580 |
| Oregon | Holy Cross Catholic School | Portland | 237,718 |
| Pennsylvania | Bridge Valley Elementary School | Furlong | 1,784,986 |
| Rhode Island | Halliwell Memorial Elem School | North Smithfield | 469,419 |
| South Carolina | Oakridge Elementary School | Clover | 137,064 |
| South Dakota | Castlewood School | Castlewood | 31,152 |
| Tennessee | Crosswind Elementary School | Collierville | 718,583 |
| Texas | Carroll Academy | Houston | 3,678,753 |
| Utah | Freedom Academy | Provo | 65,195 |
| Vermont | Calais Elementary School | Plainfield | 42,374 |
| Virginia | Ashburn Elementary School | Ashburn | 1,500,831 |
| Washington | Highlands Elementary School | Renton | 284,005 |
| West Virginia | St. Francis Central Catholic School | Morgantown | 824,560 |
| Wisconsin | Riverdale Elem School | Muscoda | 198,968 |
| Wyoming | Little Snake River Valley School | Baggs | 182,269 |

# TOP LIBRARIES AND COMMUNITY PARTNERS

New for 2017, Scholastic welcomed libraries and community partners to participate. Congratulations to the top five libraries and top five community partners that logged their summer reading minutes!

### Libraries

| | |
|---|---|
| Cobb County Library | Marietta, GA |
| Sykesville Public Library | Sykesville, PA |
| Smyrna Public Library | Smyrna, GA |
| Pickford Community Library | Pickford, MI |
| Horsham Township Library | Horsham, PA |

### Community Partners

| | |
|---|---|
| Girl Scouts of Central Maryland, Troop 2825 | Bel Air, MD |
| America Reads-Mississippi | Jackson, MS |
| QD Learning | Anaheim, CA |
| Hollywood Community Housing | Los Angeles, CA |
| Torrey Smith Family Fund | Rockville, MD |

# MILLION MINUTE READERS CLUB

In addition to the "Best in State" schools, students at these schools reached one million minutes.

| School | City | Minutes |
|---|---|---|
| Gray Elementary School | Houston, TX | 1,976,112 |
| Kujawa Elementary School | Houston, TX | 1,625,102 |
| H.D. Hilley Elementary School | El Paso, TX | 1,581,941 |
| Horizon Heights Elementary School | Horizon City, TX | 1,576,499 |
| South Elementary School | Trappe, PA | 1,353,913 |
| Skippack Elementary School | Collegeville, PA | 1,312,516 |
| Kyrene Del Cielo Elementary School | Chandler, AZ | 1,099,132 |
| Stephens Elementary School | Houston, TX | 1,097,339 |
| Rawsonville Elementary School | Ypsilanti, MI | 1,055,827 |

SCHOLASTIC.COM/SUMMER

# THE SUMMER READING CHALLENGE GOES VIRAL!

Thousands of kids were excited about reading over the summer—and about choosing what they wanted to read. Check out these cool events, stats, and viral moments from the Challenge!

One school from each state received books for their students to kick off summer as part of **The Dav Pilkey Summer Reading Educator Contest**. Here are a few of the schools celebrating their new books:

Hanceville Elementary School, Hanceville, AL

Salem Lutheran School, Affton, MO

Hualapai Elementary School, Kingman, AZ

**The Scholastic Summer Reading Road Trip** toured the country visiting communities big and small, featuring favorite authors, illustrators, and characters. The 25+ city tour included more than 50 events, visiting local bookstores, schools, and libraries across the country. Two RVs traveled a combined 10,000 miles!

## Principals Lead the Challenge

**1,500,000 MINUTES**

Ryan Stanson-Marsh, principal at Skippack Elementary School, and David D'Andrea, principal at South Elementary School, used the Scholastic Summer Reading Challenge to inspire their students to read more over the summer. They asked students to read 1.5 million minutes and announced the challenge in a video broadcast to both schools. Kids responded and blasted through the goal, reading more than 2 million minutes.

## Show Us Your Reading Adventure!

The "Show Us Your Reading Adventure" sweepstakes was a big hit! We asked to see what a reading adventure looks like to families. Two lucky winners were chosen each week in July to receive a reading prize pack full of books, posters, bookmarks, and some more goodies!

photo @motherofpearl81

photo @mommacarper

photo @felinajoy

photo @chillygoodman

## Scholastic Summer Reading Ambassadors

The First Gentleman of Oregon, Dan Little, a Scholastic Summer Reading Ambassador, paid a visit to Milwaukie Elementary School.

Arizona First Lady Angela Ducey, a Scholastic Summer Reading Ambassador, visited Francisco Vasquez de Coronado Elementary School.

New York Lt. Governor Kathy Hochul, a Scholastic Summer Reading Ambassador, visited Clara Barton School in Rochester.